PRAISE FOR *BREATHE A*

"Stacy invites us into an inspirational journey of wrestling with God to discover the beauty that emerges from a broken heart. If you've experienced devastating loss with nothing left to give, this book is for you. May you draw strength in these pages of the promise that is to come."

—REBEKAH LYONS, BESTSELLING AUTHOR OF
RHYTHMS OF RENEWAL AND *YOU ARE FREE*

"Stacy's story is like a beautiful and fragrant rose blooming out of cement because she discovered living hope and tangible peace in emotional territory others have castigated as a barren wasteland. The fact that she's been able to weave her experience with compelling biblical narrative in a way that helps others hang on to genuine joy and divine purpose while navigating dark valleys is a true gift. This must-read book is both a love letter to our Creator Redeemer and an excellent trail guide for His image bearers!"

—LISA HARPER, AUTHOR OF *THE SACRAMENT OF
HAPPY, BELIEVING JESUS*, AND MORE

"My wife, Debbie, and I are honored to call Casey and Stacy Henagan longtime friends, and we have personally witnessed them walking out the principles found in this book. Watching Stacy battle to hold on to her faith in the aftermath of losing her daughter and refusing to remain stuck in her grief, doubt, and disappointment has been both remarkable and inspiring. If you're struggling with your faith, this book will help you recognize truth and encourage you to hold on to your faith while discovering God is trustworthy and good, even when we don't understand."

—ROBERT MORRIS, FOUNDING LEAD SENIOR PASTOR AT
GATEWAY CHURCH AND BESTSELLING AUTHOR OF *THE
BLESSED LIFE, BEYOND BLESSED*, AND *TAKE THE DAY OFF*

"When Stacy Henagan endured the loss of her precious baby daughter to a terminal disease, she faced the limits of her faith in God. *Breathe Again* is her honest and inspiring account of her journey through grief, anguish, and heartache, but it is also a field guide for anyone who struggles with suffering in this world. Tracing the footsteps of Abraham's father, Terah, who also lost a child, Stacy unexpectedly discovers a new path to God's comfort, healing, and strength."

—CHRIS HODGES, SENIOR PASTOR OF CHURCH OF THE HIGHLANDS AND AUTHOR OF *THE DANIEL DILEMMA* AND *WHAT'S NEXT?*

"We all get knocked down, but how do we find the strength to get back up again? With authenticity and courage, Stacy tells her own knockdown story and how she overcame. *Breathe Again* is the encouragement you need to get back up again."

—TABATHA CLAYTOR, COLEAD PASTOR AT ALIVE CHURCH

"I was privileged to be Stacy Henagan's pastor when she and her husband, Casey, walked through the tremendous trial with Haven's life. They were full of faith, hope, and love. Their hearts were broken, but their faith was unbroken. God has rewarded them a hundredfold with an amazing church and family. If you are in a desperate situation, get ready for an amazing story of courage. Courage is even sweeter when you read about its reward."

—LARRY STOCKSTILL, TEACHING PASTOR AT BETHANY CHURCH, FOUNDER OF PASTORS UNIVERSITY, AND AUTHOR OF *MODEL MAN* AND *THE REMNANT*

"Grief, a natural expression in this life, serves to either paralyze us or make us strong. I have lived to see Stacy's amazing resilience, from devastation to powerful ministry, as she has chosen to be made strong. Her story will elevate and challenge you."

—MELANIE STOCKSTILL, FORMER COPASTOR AT BETHANY CHURCH

BREATHE AGAIN

CHOOSING TO BELIEVE THERE'S MORE
WHEN LIFE HAS LEFT YOU BROKEN

STACY HENAGAN

EMANATE
BOOKS

Published in Nashville, Tennessee, by Emanate Books, an imprint of Thomas Nelson. Emanate Books and Thomas Nelson are registered trademarks of HarperCollins Christian Publishing, Inc.

Thomas Nelson titles may be purchased in bulk for educational, business, fundraising, or sales promotional use. For information, please e-mail SpecialMarkets@ThomasNelson.com.

Unless otherwise noted, Scripture quotations are taken from The Holy Bible, New International Version®, NIV®. Copyright © 1973, 1978, 1984, 2011 by Biblica, Inc.® Used by permission of Zondervan. All rights reserved worldwide. www.Zondervan.com. The "NIV" and "New International Version" are trademarks registered in the United States Patent and Trademark Office by Biblica, Inc.®

Scripture quotations marked TPT are taken from The Passion Translation®. Copyright © 2017, 2018 by Passion & Fire Ministries, Inc. Used by permission. All rights reserved. ThePassionTranslation.com.

Scripture quotations marked ESV are taken from the ESV® Bible (The Holy Bible, English Standard Version®). Copyright © 2001 by Crossway, a publishing ministry of Good News Publishers. Used by permission. All rights reserved.

Scripture quotations marked NLT are taken from the Holy Bible, New Living Translation. © 1996, 2004, 2015 by Tyndale House Foundation. Used by permission of Tyndale House Publishers, Inc., Carol Stream, Illinois 60188. All rights reserved.

Scripture quotations marked NLV are taken from the New Life Version. © Christian Literature International.

Scripture quotations marked NRSV are taken from the New Revised Standard Version Bible. Copyright © 1989 National Council of the Churches of Christ in the United States of America. Used by permission. All rights reserved worldwide.

Any internet addresses, phone numbers, or company or product information printed in this book are offered as a resource and are not intended in any way to be or to imply an endorsement by Thomas Nelson, nor does Thomas Nelson vouch for the existence, content, or services of these sites, phone numbers, companies, or products beyond the life of this book.

ISBN 978-0-7852-3435-7 (TP)
ISBN 978-0-7852-3436-4 (eBook)

Library of Congress Control Number: 2020934307

Printed in the United States of America

20 21 22 23 24   LSC   10 9 8 7 6 5 4 3 2 1

For my husband, Casey, who reminds me what
authentic and selfless love really is.
For my kids Holland, Hayes, and Hudson,
who are my greatest reward.
For Ashton Duggar, because, well, you know why.
Finally, for Haven, who I await to join
with indescribable anticipation.

CONTENTS

PROLOGUE

It was the nineteenth of October. The time was ten twenty-five at night. The hum of the oxygen machine droned on in our bedroom. I noticed a change in my daughter's blank expression and felt an urgency to hold her. This wasn't something we did often because moving caused her discomfort.

My husband carefully laid Haven's tiny body on a pillow in my lap as I sat in a rocking chair. I could tell she was fighting for life. All I wanted to do in that moment was tell her I loved her. Over and over I told her. My mother heart had already been pulverized into tiny pieces, and I didn't know how much more it could take.

Finally I said the most honest prayer I could formulate with words. It was risky and desperate. I sat as still as I could, careful not to jostle her. I spoke no truer words than these: "God, we've given You every opportunity to heal Haven. I've given it all I have. I have no regrets because I know I have believed You as best as I know how. I have fought the good fight of faith. But Jesus, I can't stand to watch the suffering any longer. My heart hurts, but I release Haven to You. If You're not going to heal her, as hard as this is to say, please take her now."

An exhale of relief escaped from my lungs as I surrendered my will to God. I let go—not of His ability to heal my daughter, but of what I wanted. For the first time I released the outcome to Him. Ten months of intense spiritual warfare, joy and pain, light and darkness, death and life, heaven and hell culminated in this one moment. Haven was in His hands. Whether she lived or died was His to decide.

Two minutes later she exhaled her last breath in my arms.

INTRODUCTION

ARE WE STOPPING TOO SHORT?

God has good in store for each of us, something greater than the best our minds can create. I admit, it sounds a bit like a fairy tale, doesn't it? Something the younger me could have more easily believed. As a little girl I had a wildly active imagination. My bedroom could quickly transform into a classroom by lining up a few of my tattered dolls as my students. Strawberry Shortcake inevitably became the teacher's pet, mainly because I liked the way she smelled. And it never failed that Baby Alive spent most of her day in time-out, as she had a tendency to misbehave.

As time goes on, the imagination inside most of us dulls because life forces us to become realists. And believing that God has some unthinkably good future ahead is hard, especially when we've been disappointed. But it's true: before the beginning He charted our paths, which are paved with favor and lead to a future where we can enjoy His provision, protection, and presence. But unfortunately we don't all arrive at that future. Perhaps we reject His path because it looks different than we expected.

If your life looks pale in comparison to how you dreamed of it, if you've had unexpected challenges that have left you reeling, as you read this book, I want you to know that you're not alone. In fact, you're in good company. It seems that life unexpected is part of the human experience, doesn't it? Which is why it's so important that we create a conversation about it and learn how to navigate through it. I hope we can do that together.

One of the things I love about the Bible is that it provides guidance for any of life's issues. And we can always find someone in the Word who has experienced our pain. The circumstances may not be the same, but the ache is timeless and universal. I also appreciate that God takes the time to show us not only their obedience and success but their failures too. It does me good to see that I'm not the only imperfect person; Scripture is brimming with humanity gone amiss.

Genesis 11 briefly drops the name of a somewhat obscure man in Scripture. His name was Terah, and he had a son named Abram, whom God would later rename Abraham. Terah had a dream of life in the distant land of Canaan, the place that would one day be promised to his descendants. Why Canaan? Maybe he needed a fresh start. Maybe, as a descendant of a nomadic people, he'd grown restless staying in one place for too long.

Whatever his reasons, Terah took his family from their home in Ur and started the long journey to Canaan. But something unexpected happened along the way. He lost sight of his destination and never made it to the land of his dreams. Instead, Terah and his family settled in a city along their route called Harran.[1]

So what's the big deal? It wasn't that Harran was a bad place. But it was the lesser place because it wasn't Terah's intended destiny. Sadly for him, Terah would never know how significant the land of Canaan would be for his descendants. While I am in no way suggesting that Terah was supposed to take Abraham's place as the father of our faith, I am left asking, What if? What might have happened had he continued on to the land of his dreams? Together with the rest of his family, he could have had the privilege of setting his feet on the fertile ground from which blessing would eventually flow to thousands of his descendants—and to us.

But remember, Terah didn't know what we know now. He was living the pages of Genesis instead of reading them. So, he did what seemed right to him at the time. Terah stopped short, and because he was the leader of his family, everyone else stopped too. Terah remained somewhere that should have been a temporary resting place along the way.

I've always wondered why Terah stayed in Harran. Maybe his aging joints grew tired of lugging his belongings from city to city. Perhaps he couldn't bear hearing his grandchildren ask, "Are we there yet?" one more time. Or he may have thought Harran was as good a place as any to settle for a while. These reasons are all plausible and could have played a role, but I suspect that internal emotional battles may also have sapped Terah's strength to continue.

You see, something had happened in Terah's past, in Ur, before he started his long journey. Nine simple but life-altering words stand out to me in Genesis 11:28, words full of meaning and heartache: "While his father Terah was still alive, Haran died."

It's easy to read the words in the Bible as nothing but historical facts printed in black and white, but the painful truth in those words is that Terah's youngest son, Haran, died before his time, in a culture that put immense value on male heirs. We can only imagine the heartache Terah must have experienced from this loss. It was surely devastating—and debilitating.

It has been said that the death of a child is like losing the future. Did Terah's dreams

IT HAS BEEN SAID THAT THE DEATH OF A CHILD IS LIKE LOSING THE FUTURE.

get buried beneath the rubble of his pain? Did he lose his sense of tomorrow's expectancy? Was the wind so knocked out of him that he struggled to catch his breath? Was that why he settled before he made it to his destination?

UNMET EXPECTATIONS

My first time in Colorado, I was shocked at how higher altitudes can make even walking up the stairs a difficult endeavor. Adequate oxygen is essential for endurance—and that's true of emotional oxygen as well. I know from my own experience that doubt and disappointment can drain our strength, consume our focus, and steal our very breath. When our expectations for life and God aren't met, our inward struggle may leave us so tired, confused, and frustrated that we will settle in a dry and dusty place meant only for passing through. Maybe we want to move on, but finding the strength to pick ourselves up is proving difficult, if not impossible.

When I think of the English word *settle*, I get the image of settling down as in marriage, making a home together. (The Hebrew word used in Genesis 11 can carry a similar connotation.[2]) And I wonder how many of us have become married to the wilderness experiences of our lives. Perhaps you've become one with those dry places of pain and weariness. Maybe you've given it legal rights to your life and taken its name as your identity. *Loss. Divorce. Infertility.* Often, from what I have experienced and observed, as we journey to the promises God has planted in our hearts, we may find ourselves stopped in our tracks, bewildered by the pains of life, disappointed by unmet expectations, and stuck in a place of confusion with God.

Few experiences have the power to alter our course, sometimes indefinitely, like pain and disappointment. It happens when we can't come to terms with a loss, maybe from the death of a dream or a marriage, or when we expected more out of life and suddenly the weight

FEW EXPERIENCES HAVE THE POWER TO ALTER OUR COURSE, SOMETIMES INDEFINITELY, LIKE PAIN AND DISAPPOINTMENT.

of disappointment paralyzes our feet from moving a step further. Our own Canaan, God's promised inheritance to us, our life of victory, becomes a blurry dream, a quickly evaporating picture, fading in the distance from what could have been to simply what once was.

The Big Question

Sometimes it's the small decisions we make that have the greatest impact on our future. After choosing to settle in Harran, Terah ended up dying there. In my study of Harran, I learned something profound. In Hebrew, *Harran* can mean both "parched" and "crossroads."[3] Located on a major highway in the ancient world, it was known as a well-used crossroads city. Many travelers would likely have gone through Harran to get to their destination. And when they did reach Harran, they faced a choice about which road to take.

Interesting. Harran, the name meaning "parched," is an inescapable part of life for all of us, isn't it? For Terah, what could have been a crossroads on the way to his future became his dead end.

Disappointment is an appropriate response for any kind of pain, but encasing ourselves in it is not. In Harran we will all be faced with a choice: stay put or move on. After his father's death, Abram would have to make his own decision to either complete the journey Terah had started or remain comfortable in Harran.

Because Terah stopped putting one foot in front of the other, he died in a place that paled in comparison to where he could have lived. What a pity. The challenges of desert life can be our undoing if we entangle ourselves in doubt and disappointment and focus on what is wrong about our circumstances.

Perhaps there is a little Terah inside many of us. Maybe we have settled down on the way to somewhere better. Unknowingly, we have declared marriage vows and become one with pain and disappointment. Instead of being full of promise, our faith has become parched and dry. We've settled, bought a house, picked out dishes, and tried to make a life in a place that is far less than what God intended. Instead of passing through, we've made it our end destination. Things were supposed to be different, and then they weren't. And we stand right in the middle of our own personal Harran, where we must face the questions that confront all of us at some time: What do you do when God seems to have let you down? How do you live in the face of crushing disappointment? Can you trust God when He doesn't do what you think He should have done?

THE OUTCOME OF OUR LIFE'S JOURNEY HINGES ON OUR CHOICES. THE VOICE WE LISTEN TO IN PAIN DETERMINES OUR DESTINATION.

Having walked a path similar to Terah's, I know the answer is not simple. But I also know that the outcome of our life's journey hinges on our choices. The voice we listen to in pain determines our destination. Will we incline our ear to God's voice as He guides us toward His promises? Will we keep in step with the spirit of God, moving forward as He walks alongside us? Or will we trail behind, allowing pain to be our guide and to cause us to settle for life in an emotional and spiritual climate that isn't conducive for growth?

Harran doesn't have to be a dead end for you. It can become your crossroads, your way station toward all God has in store. But, you need to know this: you don't have to arrive at a place of perfection before you move forward. I've watched firsthand as my humanity gone amiss collides with Divinity—and grace happens.

My experience is that even in the darkest of times, even when we seem to have reached the deadest of ends, if we will look up, we will be able to detect a light coming over the horizon, the spirit of God piercing through our darkness. In the beginning it may be faint, but if we focus on His light, it will grow and point the way ahead.

I don't know all you have experienced that may have caused a weary arrival in Harran. But I have been there, too, and found at my lowest of lows, when I felt as if I was suffocating under life's pain, that God helped me keep moving forward, trusting that He still has more good ahead than I could possibly imagine. I pray that as you read the words of my experience, you will hear the Holy Spirit inviting you to breathe once again.

This is our moment. God is calling us, as He called Terah's son Abraham, up out of the lesser place into the better place. Let's go there together. We'll laugh and we'll cry, but it will be good and healing.

For access to a study guide and
other resources, please visit
www.StacyHenaganBook.com.

ONE

STORM CLOUDS

"It's bad. Very bad."

My feet had barely crossed the threshold of the consulting room when the pediatric neurologist made her terse announcement. The sterile white walls began to spin around me as her voice faded out, eclipsed by a ringing in my ears. I struggled to catch my breath and felt my heartbeat rise, rapid and strong, like a racing freight train about to burst through my chest.

Knees weakening, I ordered myself to sit down, sinking onto a chair in the corner of the office with Haven. I wrapped my arms protectively around my eleven-month-old daughter, who sat quietly in my lap as I tried to make sense of what was happening.

The doctor continued to speak, but the roar in my ears drowned out what she was saying. Those first four words had effectively sucked the gravity out of the room, hurling me into a surreal state. I felt suspended above my body, maybe even suspended outside of time, and everything seemed to slow to a crawl.

To make matters worse, my husband, Casey, who had always been my steady rock, had crumbled beside me. Falling to his knees, face in his hands, he simply bawled, his mix of fear and anger befitting the way our world was turning upside down.

For a few almost reverent moments, no words were spoken. The doctor paused midsentence, giving our reeling minds time to catch up to her grim diagnosis.

I desperately wanted not to believe what I was hearing in snatches, but deep down I knew denial wouldn't change anything. I forced myself to concentrate on what the doctor was telling us.

Middle-aged, wearing a white lab coat, she was businesslike, almost brusque. "You can get through this," she said, clearly wanting to press on with the results of Haven's MRI. She had ordered the test earlier that chilly morning in January when we arrived at Our Lady of the Lake Hospital in Baton Rouge, Louisiana.

"The results show a tumor in the fourth ventricle of the brain," she continued matter-of-factly. "It is very, very large—the size of a tangerine or small lemon. She doesn't have a good chance of survival."

I willed myself to breathe calmly. *Slow breaths; slow, deep breaths*, I told myself. *This can't be real. God, make this not be real.*

How can life turn so quickly? Just a few hours earlier, my greatest concern had been pizza—finding someone to make a Domino's run for the youth meeting we were scheduled to lead at our church that evening. Now pizza was inconsequential.

HOW CAN LIFE TURN SO QUICKLY? My heart went in all directions, and my thoughts couldn't keep up. With every passing minute my mind was more scattered. The doomed feeling in my gut spoke what my mind couldn't. *Am I going to lose her? Surely God wouldn't allow that to happen. How will I survive if I lose her?*

I knew I needed to keep God in my line of sight, or this crisis would eclipse everything around me. But as I glanced down at Haven, with her head resting on my chest, the fear became almost overwhelming. It was hard to comprehend that a monster tumor had been silently choking out her life.

My mind struggled between faith and fear. As if in a relentless boxing match, I was being hit from all sides, and it felt as though I was losing. I tried hard, so hard, to keep my mind set on God's faithfulness, but I kept hearing the tumor taunt, *I'm going to win. I am bigger, stronger, and fiercer than anything you know. You're going to lose your daughter, and it will destroy you.*

Dressed in her little gray leopard-print sweater and black patent-leather boots, Haven was calm in my lap, as if she was gauging our reactions.

"I'm not sure how much longer she has to live," the doctor went on. "We'll need the advice of a pediatric neurosurgeon to tell us more."

Immediately I began to cross-examine myself, because isn't that what mothers do? *How did I let this happen? Was it something I did—or did not do?* My pregnancy had been trouble-free, and I had been so diligent in taking care of myself. I took all my prenatal vitamins and avoided caffeine. I drank orange juice whenever I ate chicken because I had read somewhere that citrus helps you absorb more protein.

Maybe I had stopped breastfeeding too soon. Haven had never learned to latch on well, so nursing her had been painful and taken forever. On top of that, my social personality had chafed at being stuck behind closed doors for an hour at a time. So I'd decided it was safe to stop nursing at six weeks. Now I regretted not being more disciplined, worrying that perhaps I had made the wrong choice and shaming myself for being so selfish.

Part of me knew this line of thinking was irrational, but I couldn't seem to shake the fear. What if I had caused this? I couldn't live with that guilt, but I felt as if I needed something, someone to blame, some way of making sense of this nightmare. The room began to spin, and I shut my eyes and thought back to our first days with our precious daughter, not even a year ago.

―――――

The night before Haven's arrival, we had hurried to Woman's Hospital in Baton Rouge, making the twenty-minute drive from home soon after the first labor pains began. I may have been health conscious, but I was not into natural childbirth. I'm not a fan of pain, to say the least. And as I was clueless about how slow first-time labor usually is, I didn't want to get there just to have the doctor tell me I was too far along to get an epidural.

As it turned out, I had nothing to worry about. It would be twelve long hours after we got to the hospital before our firstborn would weigh in at a healthy seven pounds, fourteen ounces. And the miracle everyone tells you will happen when you meet your child for the first time definitely happened to me. The second I laid eyes on that chubby, wrinkled face, something inside me changed. My heart seemed to burst open like a flowering bud, enlarging with a capacity for love that I didn't know I could possess.

We named her Haven because the name means "refuge." Our prayer was that her life would point people to God, in whom they could find ultimate shelter. Little did we know the ways her life would embody those words in the months that followed.

With a small army of doctors and nurses buzzing around, I marveled at how someone so small could so easily command a room. I quickly realized that even more so after our first week at home, when

I no longer knew what sleep was. So many nights with so little sleep. Yet our bloodshot eyes and zombielike minds in those first weeks of parenthood couldn't diminish the promise I felt as I looked forward to Haven's future.

Back then, life had been so good. Working jobs we loved as student pastors, surrounded by friends we enjoyed, Casey and I had been rich with youthful optimism, the kind that makes you feel ten feet tall and bulletproof. The sky had truly seemed to be the limit.

But then, just three weeks ago, my safe utopia had crumbled. And now the sky was falling.

On Christmas night—of all nights—Haven had thrown up as I was putting her to bed. Babies get sick, of course, so I wasn't really worried at the time. We had been to five Christmas parties in two days and spent Christmas Day with lots of family. *Maybe she picked up a virus at one of those gatherings*, I had thought. *Or maybe the chocolate cake I saw my aunt feeding her earlier had upset her stomach.*

But the vomiting continued the next day, and the next, then every day, multiple times a day, for three weeks. By then I had begun to panic. My mind was spinning out of control imagining every horrific possibility. I needed answers.

We visited two pediatricians and an ear, nose, and throat specialist. None of them could identify what the problem was, despite running multiple tests. But they all assured us that there was nothing serious to worry about.

I had wanted to believe the doctors' words were true and that everything was okay, but there was this nagging feeling—maybe it was mother's intuition or maybe it was just fear. But something in me knew that if I believed the doctors' words, I'd be lying to myself. I had hardly let my mind go there, but every day I became more unable to keep the worry tamped down. Haven was becoming increasingly lethargic, content only when I was holding her, and she also appeared to be losing her balance, falling onto her right side every time she crawled. *Was this an inner-ear problem? Was there something wrong with her muscles?* I had thought. I was scared, and my fear had made me frustrated and angry, causing me to erupt at the slightest situation because no one could give me solid answers.

After that, my fears had been heightened when the ENT doctor inserted tubes in Haven's ears, hoping that might resolve the problem. In the recovery room after the outpatient procedure, Haven had taken a long time to come out of anesthesia and when she did finally become alert, she was difficult to console. Nothing I did eased her crying.

At one point, when I had tried to calm her with a pacifier, something that had always worked before, Haven had taken it and thrown it across the room. At first I had assumed such irritability was normal for babies after surgery. Then I glimpsed a momentary expression of concern flash across the face of one of the attending nurses. No one else had noticed, but I caught it. It was as if in that millisecond, she had silently spoken to me: *This is serious.*

As soon as we got home after being released from the surgery center, Haven vomited again. The tubes weren't working. I was at a loss—and so was my peace. That intuitive voice that I had fiercely tried to ignore urged me to keep pursuing answers. But I was terrified I might discover there was something gravely wrong with Haven, that a world of pain might open up and our lives would never be the same.

I worked hard to ignore the voice, even though muffling its rising volume was causing me anxiety—shaky hands, a quivering voice, and pent-up tears that were ready to flow free at a moment's notice. I feared admitting that Haven could be gravely sick. It seemed that once I released those words into the atmosphere, I could never get them back. So, I kept on denying what I suspected to be true, hoping the denial would make it all go away. But you cannot pray effectively for something you won't admit is broken. You can't believe God for something you pretend doesn't need a miracle. Every day you choose not to acknowledge what's really going on is another day without a solution.

I couldn't deny my suspicions any longer, so I pressed Haven's pediatrician to arrange a consultation with a pediatric neurologist. Her response struck me like a hard fist, making me wish I could take back my request. "I'm just letting you know that this could open up a can of worms," she said. "I want you to be prepared."

I had hung up the phone in a daze and repeated the one word I knew could help me the most: *Jesus, Jesus, Jesus.* The response to my cry was a peace that we were pointed in the right direction.

The consulting room finally stopped spinning, and I opened my eyes again. I felt numb, body and soul. I sat frozen in the metal chair, staring dully at the faded and picked blue carpet.

We had arrived at Our Lady of the Lake Hospital just this morning knowing that we were likely facing something serious but holding out hope that by some miracle our appointment would rule out real trouble, not reveal it. No more than ten minutes in, the neurologist had sent us downstairs for an immediate MRI. The nurse had grabbed my mother-in-law's arm and whispered, "Good luck." She knew. But really, hadn't we all? Denial had just suppressed our potential for pain.

But here it was, bubbling to the surface.

As much as I wanted to cry uncontrollably, I couldn't. I needed some way to lance the devastating pain that was ballooning inside me, but the flood of tears refused to come. And that shamed me. Why wasn't I bawling? What kind of mother was I?

Maybe I was in shock. I remembered getting in a car accident as a teenager and feeling the same way—numb, distant, as if my surroundings weren't real. It was almost as though I was off to one side, watching myself.

But there might have been another reason for my lack of reaction. I was also seven months pregnant with our second—and surprise—daughter. Already emotional and tired from the baby I was carrying in my arms and the one I was carrying inside me, maybe I just didn't have the capacity to feel anything more.

Whatever was behind my fog, it was a gift of some sort because, at least for now, I didn't have to face the feelings that defied expression, the emotions that threatened to crush the life out of me and bury me beneath them.

The doctor leaned against her desk, carefully gauging my reactions. I could read pity in her eyes, and I despised it. I felt exposed and helpless and overwhelmingly vulnerable; this crisis was so far beyond the scope of my control.

As much as I hate to admit it, I like control because it gives me a sense of security. It tells me that whatever I have a tight grip on is safe. Sure, I may be squeezing the life out of it, but it gives me a sense of power and that temporarily relieves my anxiety. In my heart I know this isn't true. I know my grasp is fallible and lacking, and I also know that my only true safety comes when I release my grip and depend on the ability of God. Yet something in me still resists letting go. Something in me finds it hard to trust.

As we sat with the doctor, I knew that it was impossible, even with my best effort, for me to change this brain tumor diagnosis. There was nothing I could do, and that's a terrible feeling. Yet in the midst of this helplessness was a voice I recognized. It was small, steady, and somewhere down deep. It was hope, keeping me upright like an anchor inside. Constant but never shouting. Strong but tender. Ready but not demanding. This hope pointed me to Jesus and kept whispering His name.

There are times when, though they seem like strangers, hope and helplessness reside right next to each other in the human heart. On the one hand, we long to believe that God will do a miracle, that He has complete control. On the other, we feel helpless that things may never change, that what we face might be too big for God's ability.

I've seen myself reflected many times in the distraught face of the father mentioned in Mark 9. He cried out to Jesus in anguish over his son, who had been tormented by Satan for years. He was a good dad. He wanted to help his son, so he begged Jesus, "If you can do anything . . . help" (v. 22).

THERE ARE TIMES WHEN, THOUGH THEY SEEM LIKE STRANGERS, HOPE AND HELPLESSNESS RESIDE RIGHT NEXT TO EACH OTHER IN THE HUMAN HEART.

Like many of life's situations, this was bigger than the father's capacity, and he couldn't find anyone with enough ability to help him. As He always does when we ask, Jesus stepped in for this father. He didn't panic. He simply took control. He knew He had authority over demonic spirits, but hearing the father's unbelieving heart, He wanted the man to learn to trust Him. Knowing this wouldn't be the only moment of need in this father's life, Jesus wanted to teach him to have faith. So He told the father, "If you are able to believe, all things are possible to the believer" (v. 23 TPT).

The man's response was exactly what Jesus was looking for: "I do believe, Lord; help my little faith!" (v. 24 TPT).

God's parenting is amazing, isn't it? He doesn't ask us for perfection. He simply wants a heart that is willing to trust Him: *Lord, help.* I wonder how many times I've leaned into helplessness more than hope.

I'm not sure why there are some situations where I look to God as my second or third or fourth option. Perhaps it's because I want something tactile, tangible. If I can touch it, I tend to think I can trust it. But I want to learn to be more like this father. Instead of grasping for control, I want to learn to say, "Lord, help." Not leaning on my ability but remembering that it is Jesus who is actually in control. It never fails that the more I interfere and try to control, the more I make a mess of the situation. Even when the situation is my own heart.

THE GIFT OF PRESENCE

The doctor's diagnosis, her statement that Haven didn't have long to live, reverberated in my head. Slowly a sense of clarity returned, but it was far from comforting. As the fog lifted, I woke up to the frightening reality that only a miracle could save my little girl.

As with the father in Mark 9, *Help my little faith* was my sincere cry. I believed in miracles. I had witnessed God do the seemingly impossible in my life. I'd seen Him restore family members to health and provide finances for Casey and me when we were in need. But never had I faced any trial of this magnitude, these life-or-death stakes. I fought to remember that God was present, that He had a solution, that someway, somehow, He would intervene.

Casey led the way, shaking himself out of his slump and peppering the doctor with questions about what was next and when and how and why.

We were told that Haven would be admitted to the hospital right away; she needed surgery as soon as possible. The tumor was so large in her small skull that it was causing hydrocephalus, a buildup of spinal fluid that put immense pressure on the brain. That was the culprit behind her vomiting and loss of balance. Untreated, it would soon kill her.

We were admitted to the children's floor of the hospital. A nurse there gave me a tiny hospital gown for Haven to wear. It was bright and colorful, with balloons printed on it. Just the day before I would have thought it was cute. But not now. I despised everything it represented, and I wanted to go home.

The nurse pointed to a box on a shelf in the corner of the room. "If Haven stops breathing, we will use the drill in that box to put a hole in her head to relieve the fluid on her brain," she told me. I must have looked as white as a sheet, because the nurse continued, "We don't anticipate that, but I needed you to know."

And then the room began spinning again.

Staring at the box on the shelf, I nearly gave in to the panic. With so many unknowns, the what-ifs consumed my mind. *What if I can't endure this? What if this tumor damages Haven's brain permanently? What if it takes her life?*

With nothing to distract me, fear was rising. I needed words of encouragement, the familiar touch of someone who loved me, someone to look straight into my eyes and speak words of faith to me. Thank God we serve a Savior who anticipates our needs before we feel them and already has a plan.

THANK GOD WE SERVE A SAVIOR WHO ANTICIPATES OUR NEEDS BEFORE WE FEEL THEM AND ALREADY HAS A PLAN.

Within a short time after Haven was admitted, family and friends began to arrive. Teary-eyed sisters, brothers, parents, friends, and pastors surrounded us, encouraging us not to give up hope. If we were floating at sea, clinging to a capsized boat, then the Coast Guard had just appeared for us. And just the sight of that help created a surge of hope in me: *I can do this.*

I am not alone. God has made me strong, and there are people around who love me. With each person who entered the room, I exhaled a little more, breathing a little more calmly. Simply knowing we were surrounded by so many loved ones was like a shot of endurance in my arm.

By five that evening, several hundred people had gathered in the hall outside our hospital room. I could hear the commotion and wondered when the nurses would order everyone to leave. I was hoping they would put up with the craziness as long as possible, because the visitors' presence was helping me.

It was comforting and encouraging to experience such care and concern from so many people. There were moments when their company would take my mind off my crisis and I'd almost believe that life was normal again. I'd be laughing among friends, and my heart would feel momentarily free. But then reality would suddenly hit me. I would remember that Haven had a brain tumor the size of a lemon in the back of her head and that the doctor had said she would probably die. Then panic and dread would once again seize my heart.

I had no idea how to handle a crisis like this publicly, even in front of these people who loved me. *Do I let go and completely fall apart in front of everyone?* If I did, I wasn't sure I would be able to recover. I knew no one really expected me to be Wonder Woman, but I wasn't ready to be so vulnerable in my pain. So, I projected a brave face, while underneath the apparent courage I was frightened to death.

In a matter of a few hours, everything in my world had shifted. Instead of getting dressed for that night's youth service, I sat in a hospital room as the crowd thinned and people went home. They left us with prayers and love and, thanks to my mother, clean clothes.

That day I appreciated my church family as never before. They rose to the occasion, giving us slips of papers on which they had written Scripture verses and leaving devotional books to bring encouragement. Some brought food, while others shoved money into our pockets. Though no one could take away our pain, they stood with us in it, and that was enough to make me not feel alone.

IN THE STILLNESS

Finally, long hours after we were admitted, the hospital floor grew quiet and the lights in our room were dimmed. I sat in a rocking chair with Haven on my lap as Casey rested against the side of her hospital bed. Lost for words, we did not speak. I could hear Casey praying under his breath. A stillness filled the air. A reprieve from all the noise of the previous hours should have been welcome, but I suddenly wanted the rush of people again. Without the movement and chaos, the fears I had fought to suppress now surged to the surface, and it was hard to face them.

The questions sneaked out around the barrier I had tried to erect. *If Haven lives, will she be normal? Will I be able to endure the long road ahead and face whatever happens? Why is this happening to me?*

Forced into stillness and relative solitude, I struggled to maintain my composure, but my pent-up emotions demanded release. The tears I had tried so hard to muster during the day now wouldn't stop flowing. Unchecked, they coursed down my cheeks onto Haven's tiny body.

More minutes of deafening silence passed. Then, like a deep and resonant bell of hope and faith, Casey's voice rang through my grief.

"We're not giving up on God." It was a statement, a declaration—bold, firm, resolute.

He sounded different from the devastated father who hours earlier had been knocked to his knees. Now his voice was steady, strong, and unwavering as he looked into my eyes.

"Even if things don't go our way, even if this road is long and, God forbid, we lose her—if God doesn't heal her—we are not turning our backs on Him," he said. "We've come too far to turn back now. Stacy, God has been too good, too faithful, and I choose to trust Him for her healing. Are you with me?"

TWO

TRUSTING FORWARD

*Never be afraid to trust an unknown
future to a known God.*
Corrie ten Boom

"Will you trust God?" Casey asked me. I knew my answer would determine how I fought this battle that had suddenly been waged against me.

Would I trust God? Could I? Of course I wanted to, but it was going to be hard. This was no normal situation, and I knew this kind of trust was impossible on my own. I needed supernatural help. And to access that help, I needed to draw close to my heavenly Father.

Hidden in Casey's words was God's divine call to meet with Him. To traverse the hill on which He sits overlooking our lives and connect heart to heart, soul to soul. It's not a ritual. It's a lifeline. And here's the beautiful thing: before I knew this trial was coming, God had prepared a table with the sustenance I would need. When Haven's diagnosis crushed me, He invited me to dine with Him.

I had a decision to make at that point, and it would either become my dead end or a crossroads on the way to my future. I could either stay put in broken dreams and confusion or pull up a chair to His table.

An invitation has been sent to you as well; your name is written on it. The table He's prepared for you has everything you need. The fruit was grown in the vineyard of His Spirit, and the meat was carved from His Word. Tasting it is how you will learn to trust.

In every crisis, every deferred dream, every disappointment, is an invitation to meet with God. Pain or possibility—that's our choice. But we won't become the people God has destined us to be, we won't weather the storms of life in the way He intends, until we say yes to His invitation.

It's no mystery how to be happy when life is going well. No one has to teach us how to trust God when we get the job, when our bank account is overflowing, when the guy finally asks us on the date, or when our marriage is better than ever. Trust is easy during good times. Joy is abundant.

I haven't heard many sermons on how to endure great days or listened to podcasts on how to overcome disappointment when God answers your prayer right away. This is not where the tension is. This is not where our questions lie. These are not the things that jar our faith and make us question our theology, what we really believe to be true about God.

IT IS WHEN OUR PAIN AND OUR THEOLOGY COLLIDE THAT WE MOST NEED REAL ANSWERS AND SOLID TRUTH.

It's the rumble of pain that moves through us like an earthquake. It's when God doesn't do what we expect Him to do. It's when our experience seems to violently oppose the truth that we built our life upon—when we don't get the healing, when the business goes bankrupt, or when divorce papers are served.

It is when our pain and our theology collide that we most need real answers and solid truth. And it's while we're searching for those answers and that truth that the call comes for us to meet with God—not for explanation, but for loving connection. It is in that space that we discover the truth that if we have trust, then we don't need explanation.

OPPORTUNITIES

The longer we are on the earth, the more opportunities we will have to put our hearts in God's hands, to rely on His power, and to believe that He won't disappoint us. These opportunities are most often packaged in the form of crisis, challenge, or pain. We can either despise them or see them as a chance to expand our trust in Him, to experience His presence and provision in deeper ways than before.

Sometimes marriages fail, kids rebel, sickness creeps in, and company positions are eliminated. Sometimes we pray for a situation to have a specific outcome and God doesn't do what we ask. We can be sure that not everything in life will go as planned, but I know I'm not telling you anything you haven't experienced firsthand. The chasm between our unmet expectation and our present reality can be a birthing place for doubt and disappointment, which in turn will tempt us to distrust the goodness and power of God. Maybe I should rephrase that and say that it *will* create disappointment, which can tempt us to doubt the goodness and power of God.

Disappointment is simply a given in this broken world. We can blame it on all sorts of things, but sin is at its root. Our heartache can be a consequence of our sin, the fallout of someone else's, or simply the by-product of living in a fallen world, where sin so dominantly exists.

It would be so nice if everyone got along, if disease were non-existent, if there was no such thing as cellulite. Am I right? That's exactly what life was like for the first two people God created, before they made the fatal choice to disobey God. Okay, who knows if there was cellulite, but we are so far removed from how the world first started that it's hard to even imagine. No one was ever supposed to be depressed or lonely. Sickness had no access to anyone's body. Grief was unheard of. There was no war, abuse, poverty, racism, no worry or doubt. And absolutely no brain tumors!

Pain simply wasn't part of God's plan for humanity. If we want to know why disappointment exists, then we must understand His original intent for us. And we don't have to look any further than creation. The earth was perfectly balanced, and the environment in the garden of Eden was safe and nurturing. Adam and Eve had direct access and constant connection to God's presence. Everything they needed—physically, spiritually, and emotionally—was provided for.

But the world changed the day God's first two children made a decision to distrust Him because Satan had convinced them that God was withholding goodness. The irony was that they had no valid reason *not* to trust. With no prior pain to use as evidence, why would they doubt His intentions toward them?

I guess I can answer that by my own experiences with doubting Him and say that Satan is cunning, isn't he? He's a mastermind at twisting spiritual truths into legalism and lies.

While tragedy was always one disobedient decision away, those first humans lived within a hedge of innocence that protected them from it. But deciding to ponder Satan's accusation of God placed their feet over the protective hedge and opened them up to a world of disappointment—and worse. Once innocence was lost, the darkness of sin grew in the human heart like a rapidly spreading virus. Then came the consequence of death—our new inheritance—which, as author Randy Alcorn put it, tore apart "what God created and joined together. God intended for our bodies to last as long as our souls."[1]

Have you ever wanted to take someone by the shoulders and shake sense into them? That's what I want to do to Adam and Eve whenever I contemplate what they did back in the garden. *Why didn't you just trust that God was good and trustworthy?* I want to say. *Do you see the pain I'm going through because of your decision?* And yet I can't deny that I see my reflection in their regretful faces and recognize my own humanity in their compromise. The truth is, I might have done the same thing. How many times have *I* mistrusted God when I, too, have direct access to Him by His own Spirit living within me?

Like Adam and Eve, you and I are susceptible to the voice of God's accuser, which echoes resoundingly in our pain. Like a thief, that voice comes to steal our trust in Him and cause us to question His character. *Is God even trustworthy?* we may wonder. *If He is, then why is this happening to me?* If we're not careful, we may be left picking up the broken pieces of our lives, lost in our pain and confusion, trying to figure out how to deal with our disappointments and to climb out of the valley between our unmet expectations and reality. We may even push aside the very One who can get us out of the mess because our hearts cannot shake the suspicion that He can't be trusted.

What went down in the garden of Eden was terrible, and I wish it had never happened. But here is some theology we can build our lives upon: At the very moment when sin entered the human heart, even as heaven wept over what had been lost, God lit a fire of hope in the world. Like a spark in dry leaves, fanned by the Holy Spirit, it smoldered in the hearts of men and women through the ages until the day of Christ's arrival, when it burst into full blaze.

Wow. What a gift we've been given. Jesus' death and resurrection provide the redemptive remedy to our sin problem and every negative effect it has caused. When Jesus rose from the grave, as C. S. Lewis so eloquently put it, "death itself [started] working backwards."[2] The curse of sin was broken for good. Defeated. Completely eradicated.

And yet the odor of sin still lingers, doesn't it? Every time something bad happens, I smell it. Every time I'm let down, I get a whiff. Jesus' work is complete, but we won't see the full reality of it until we breathe our last breath or He comes to rapture us home. Until the day Jesus recreates this world and makes all things new, sin and death remain part of our habitation, which means there will be times when this broken world will break us. But like Adam and Eve, we all have a choice to make. Will we sit at God's table and learn to trust Him when everything falls apart, even when we don't understand Him?

Not Exempt

You're not alone if you don't understand God's ways. When Casey asked me to trust God with him, I struggled to process the reality that while God didn't cause the brain tumor, He did allow it to form. And He let that terrible thing happen to *us*. Casey and I were pastors who spent our days trying to convince teenagers whose frontal lobes hadn't yet developed to stop being rebellious and to live for God. We put in countless hours of work for a small salary out of devotion to God and those teenagers. Now I found myself questioning if that counted for anything.

Did you ever take a test in high school that would exempt you from the final exam if you passed it? I probably wouldn't have recognized it during this trial, but in the back of my mind, I assumed that my good works worked that way, that they somehow exempted me from this sort of tragedy. Sounds arrogant, I know, but don't most of us make this kind of assumption? When trouble hits and we ask why it's happening to us, isn't that a sign that we expected it *not* to happen because deep down we felt exempt?

That's when we find ourselves in our own personal Harran, overwhelmed with heartache and disappointed with the realization that we weren't exempt after all.

ADVERSITY BRINGS US ALL, EVENTUALLY, TO THE CROSSROADS OF DISAPPOINTMENT AND TRUST.

Adversity brings us all, eventually, to the crossroads of disappointment and trust. Disappointment because life isn't what we expected. And trust because God is calling us to follow Him, blindly, out of our confusion, disillusionment, and fear. At my crossroads of decision, I wanted to trust God all the way to the promised land, but I was learning that desire is not all it takes.

TRUSTING ENOUGH TO JUMP

"I've got you—now jump!" I can still hear Casey repeating those words to each of our kids when they were younger. Their pudgy toddler feet were fixed on the kitchen counter as he'd back away, coaxing them to leap into his arms. Though he stood only a foot away, in their eyes it might as well have been a mile. Their wide grins and laughter were evidence that they wanted to make the jump, but the fear of falling kept them planted. "Trust me. I'm going to catch you," he'd repeat until they worked up enough nerve to believe him. Eventually, after lots of coaxing and several false starts, they'd bravely abandon their fear and launch like little flying squirrels into their daddy's waiting arms. For each kid, the thought pattern was the same: *I'm scared. Dad reassures me. I believe Dad. Here goes nothing! . . . Dad caught me. Dad is true to his word. I can trust Dad. I want to jump again!*

That night in the hospital when Casey asked me to trust God, it was as if I were planted on the kitchen counter as Jesus beckoned me to leave the safety of my reasoning and jump to Him. And my thought pattern then was the same as my kids' pattern years later: *I'm scared. Jesus reassures me that He'll catch me.* And then comes the moment of decision: *I believe Him to the point that I can say, "Here goes nothing!"*

The problem is that all too often I hesitate before I get to that crucial moment. I stop before I leap. My head knows that God is faithful, but at times my heart struggles to believe. That night He met me where I was.

To trust God in a painful situation is to be vulnerable because we are not in control of the outcome. According to bestselling author and researcher Brené Brown, to be vulnerable means to face uncertainty, risk, and emotional exposure.[3] We may be uncertain of the outcome of a situation, at risk of disappointment over what God chooses for us, emotionally exposed because the situation touches on our deepest fears and emotions. But as believers we have a certainty even in our vulnerability. When we place our beating hearts into God's hands and give Him control, He vows to care for those hearts with passion and protectiveness. He won't abuse our hearts or act carelessly with them. He will never seduce or tease. And He will always choose for us the good and perfect path that brings glory to His name. So while we vulnerably trust and believe in His ability, we allow Him room to be sovereign in His choices.

The bigger the problem, the bigger the fear we must move past—and it can be so enormous that sometimes it even seems bigger than God. This is why the choice to pick up our feet to follow Jesus can't be based on desire alone. It must be combined with the belief that God is able and trustworthy.

When we struggle with trust, perhaps the biggest issue is our perception of how big and faithful God is.

HERE GOES NOTHING

"Will you trust God?"

In the dim light of the hospital room, settling like an ominous and approaching doom, the weight of fear on my shoulders kept me glued to that chair. Haven lay quietly against my swollen belly, my unborn child within. She didn't look well. Her head rested heavily on my chest. Her hospital gown and the IV hooked to her arm were visual reminders of just how sick she was. For the thousandth time that day, I caught myself holding my breath. *Inhale. Exhale.* My response to Casey's question hung in the silence.

Saying yes was the right answer. I knew the Bible inside and out, was versed in prayer, and could lead someone down the Roman Road to salvation, yet when my husband asked if I would trust God, fear crawled down my throat, snatched the word *yes*, and replaced it with *what if.* What if God didn't catch me? The chasm between His safe arms and where I stood loomed too large. There were too many unknowns, and I couldn't afford any outcome other than Haven's survival.

What if? What if I trust God but He doesn't do what I need Him to do? And here lay the root of my struggle: fear of disappointment.

What felt like hours of silence was really only seconds as I contemplated my response to Casey's question. It became impossible to ignore the stirring within, the holy beckoning to accept God's invitation. The calling was to open my heart to the God of possibilities even in the presence of fear and to jump into His invisible arms extended out to me.

God was waiting. I was standing on the counter, contemplating a leap. But the Holy Spirit in His kindness didn't leave me standing there alone. He met me where I was in my faith and drew for me a picture of what could be—beautiful sketches of peace and victory, fanning into flame a spark of hope.

I chose to launch by believing God. It wasn't perfect faith, but He never asked for that. So I gave Him what I had, imperfection and all, because I decided that life was scarier if I stayed on the counter.

"Yes, I will trust God with you. I'm scared to death, so afraid I can hardly speak, but I know He is able." Even as I said the words, my voice quivered, and tears streamed down my face.

INHALING TRUST, EXHALING FEAR

In Psalm 23 King David made the most stunning confession about how to trust God when fear is standing in the way:

> Lord, even when your path takes me through
> the valley of deepest darkness,
> fear will never conquer me, for you already have!
> You remain close to me and lead me through it all the way.
> Your authority is my strength and my peace.
> The comfort of your love takes away my fear.
> I'll never be lonely, for you are near.
> You become my delicious feast
> even when my enemies dare to fight.

You anoint me with the fragrance of your Holy Spirit;
you give me all I can drink of you until my heart overflows.
So why would I fear the future?
For your goodness and love pursue me all the days of my life.
Then afterward, when my life is through,
I'll return to your glorious presence to be forever with you!

(vv. 4–6 TPT)

We know from Scripture that David experienced more evil than most of us would know in three lifetimes. He buried several children, was betrayed by his spiritual father and sold out by his own son, faced the constant threat of murder, and was rejected by those he thought loved him. That is a lot for one man to handle. If there had been professional counseling in his day, his bill would have been astronomical. Yet even as he described walking through a dark and dangerous valley, he also told evil, "I will not fear you." Remarkable.

I don't believe for one minute that David frolicked through his dark valley making dandelion necklaces without a care in the world. He would have had to be superhuman to respond to pain without fear, and we know from reading of his mistakes that he was a real person with human tendencies just like the rest of us. I think he simply *chose* to keep walking through the valley and believe in God's faithfulness, even with the feeling of fear nipping at his heels.

That's not to say David was double-minded. I'm not sure where we got the idea that fear and trust won't ever coexist. In fact, I think this is where many of us get off track. We stop in the valley, waiting for fear to leave before we continue. But if we're waiting for the confidence to take the next step unafraid, we might as well pour concrete around our feet, because there are times when we must walk forward even in fear.

Isn't this the ultimate act of trust? When I took my leap of faith to trust God with Haven's illness, I was shaking in my shoes. But to me, that was trust. It was saying yes to God in the face of fear. And I would learn that the *feeling* of courage met me *after* I jumped, when I realized God was going to catch me.

David had a revelation while dining at God's table: his greatest pain couldn't destroy him if God was with him, even though it sure felt like it would at times. And no matter what frightening shadows the valley cast, David knew God's presence was close, leading him on the path to victory. Our lives hold this same truth.

Why was David so confident that God was with him? Because God's goodness and mercy had been in pursuit of him every moment of every hour of every day of his life. For courage to move forward, David looked to his past and remembered what the Lord had done for him.

Maybe that's a helpful practice for all of us who are learning to trust. I try to make it a habit to live in the present. But is it possible that we spend too little time remembering God's goodness in our past?

That's what I did that night in Haven's hospital room. In the hush of the late evening hour, I practiced inhaling trust and exhaling fear by shifting my focus to God's faithfulness in my yesterdays. I brought to mind the time He had spared my life in a car accident when I was fifteen. The way His tender touch felt in my heart during intimate times of worship. The miraculous way He had provided our home, which is a crazy story I'd love to tell you sometime. I recalled His past goodness until hope seeped its way into my fear for the future. I'm not saying that all the fear disappeared, but hope forced it to loosen its grip.

The sooner we practice trust, the sooner we walk in peace. I had no idea how things would end for us, but I had experienced enough of Jesus to know that He had proven Himself trustworthy.

THE SICK-CHILD CLUB

Forty-eight hours after diagnosis day, Casey, Haven, and I boarded a plane to Memphis, Tennessee, to meet with a world-renowned pediatric neurosurgeon. The electronic double doors of Le Bonheur Children's Hospital opened wide, welcoming us into a world of brightly painted walls and stimulating sights and sounds. People of all ages filled the lobby. Kids scurried around the indoor playground like little ants stirred from their mound. Weary-eyed parents pulled sick children in red wagons, while other kids wearing hospital gowns walked around attached to IV poles. Some faces looked happy, some exhausted, some angry.

The contrast between the cheery decor and the solemn look on some of the faces couldn't have been more striking. My emotions welled up inside me. I didn't want to be in this situation, in this unfamiliar hospital, and I absolutely didn't want to join this sick-child club. I refused to think that this would become my life. Refused.

Did I see myself as better than those parents and kids? No. But I didn't want to endure the pain that seemed to attach itself to them like a life-sucking leech. Feeling panic rise, I shoved away the mental images of me wearily pulling Haven in a plastic red wagon through the halls. I sat down in a chair nearby, closing my eyes to block it all away. *Breathe.*

Finally a hospital social worker retrieved us from the lobby and ushered us to our new room on the seventh floor, which I would later learn held the sickest kids in the hospital. The first things I noticed when I stepped into the room were a cold and sterile-looking metal crib in the center, one maroon chair tucked away in the corner, and a woman's voice blaring from a speaker in the wall: "Nurse Amanda is needed at the nurse's station."

Then, seconds later, another call came, this time for a different nurse. Like rapid fire, the same loud voice rang out again and again, calling for medicine, assistance, and who knows what else. It dawned on me that every call made from the nurse's station could be heard in every hospital room on the floor.

You've got to be kidding me. Who designs something like this? I wondered if the noise would go on all night. If so, how would anyone get sleep? Surely there had to be a mute button or volume control; no logical person would build a system like this without an off switch. I quickly searched the walls of the room but found nothing to silence the annoying sounds that added to the unrelenting noise in my own mind.

A half hour later I had taped a washcloth over the speaker. It didn't help muffle the noise much, but at least it made me feel as if I was telling the aggravating contraption who was boss. Since the brain-tumor diagnosis, I had felt powerless, and being the boss of my daughter's room gave me a minimal sense of control.

Soon the social worker from the lobby arrived to escort Casey and me down the hospital hall to meet with the neurosurgeon. We left Haven napping in the care of the nurses as we followed the social worker to a room the size of a walk-in closet. The neurosurgeon entered the room, and I was struck by his unkempt appearance. With shaggy hair hanging in his eyes, a wrinkled lab coat, and old, scuffed white tennis shoes, he looked a little like the eccentric scientist from *Back to the Future*. Beside him in the cramped space stood a younger and, thankfully, better groomed attendant.

We were told to sit down next to a small, round table that was littered with dozens of disorganized papers. The surgeon spoke abruptly, with very little in the way of bedside manner. "First I'm going to talk, and I want you to listen. I have a lot to get through, and I need to make sure you understand. Don't say anything or ask me any questions until I'm done. Are we all clear?"

Was I allowed to say yes? I wasn't sure, so I nodded.

For the next half hour, the surgeon spoke in detail about the statistical outcome of Haven's surgery and how he would remove the large tumor. His words were dry and emotionless as he said there was a 50 percent chance Haven would not survive the operation. "She may never wake up," he explained almost nonchalantly. "It's risky, and I will do everything in my power to keep her alive, but I can make no guarantees." As if he had just informed us of the day's weather, he went straight into the details of the surgery without pausing for my mind to process the part where he'd said my daughter *might never wake up*.

He explained he would use a machine created by NASA to guide his hands in removing the tumor. The surgery would last roughly eight hours and would likely require several blood transfusions. As if all of this wasn't enough for me to digest, he then spat out a frightening list of possibilities that had a 75 percent chance of happening to Haven. She might never learn to walk. She might spend the rest of her life breathing through a tracheostomy tube in her throat. She might never hear again. After dropping that last bombshell, he assured me that Haven could learn sign language. Maybe he was trying to suggest a bright side, but it wasn't helping.

The doctor went on to say there was also a 75 percent probability that Haven would need a permanent shunt placed in her brain to drain excess fluid and that the surgery could precipitate an alarming experience called posterior fossa syndrome. Patients with this syndrome wake from anesthesia out of sorts and inconsolable because they've lost speech, some motor skills, and possibly their memory, leaving them unable to identify people. This condition could last from days to months.

My mind struggled to keep up. *A 75 percent probability!* But the doctor was still talking. He ended by informing us that the large size of the tumor indicated it was highly likely that it was malignant, which meant Haven would probably need chemotherapy and become a patient at St. Jude Children's Research Hospital there in Memphis.

I was speechless throughout the surgeon's talk, but a geyser of emotion was building inside me. Crying, kicking, and screaming, possibly even throwing something, would have released my internal pressure valve. Unfortunately I had to remain civilized. So I breathed deeply while viciously blinking back my swelling tears.

When the doctor finished scaring me speechless with his statistics, it was our turn to speak. Casey asked questions in rapid fire. I couldn't comprehend how he had the presence of mind to formulate clear thoughts when it was taking every drop of my energy to hold myself together. This surgeon didn't seem the type to graciously handle an emotional mother, so I let my husband do all the talking. One word out of my mouth, and I had no doubt that unceasing hysteria would flow instead of intelligible words.

Shell-shocked, eyes glazed, we walked back to our hospital room after the grueling consultation. I was starting to wonder if we would ever meet with doctors and not feel traumatized. I noticed that a rollaway cot had been brought into our room. That was kind of someone. Glancing over to the crib, I saw Haven sleeping and thanked the nurse who had stayed to watch her. Casey sat down on the squeaky cot while I took the chair in the corner of the room.

Neither of us spoke. Essentially the surgeon had said that if Haven made it through surgery—and it was a strong *if*—she would have a poor quality of life. What do you say to each other after hearing those kinds of words? "It's going to be okay"? Trite statements wouldn't help.

Panic rose like burning bile in my throat. *She'll die in surgery. You're powerless.* The thought quickly took over my heart.

Only two days before, we had confessed our trust in God, but I questioned how I would walk it out when I was continually being bombarded with opportunities to retreat in fear. If only it weren't so hard to trust.

AT ALL TIMES

Trust is a common theme in the Bible, mentioned more than two hundred times. One of those is Psalm 62:8 (ESV), which urges:

> Trust in him at all times, O people;
>> pour out your heart before him;
>> God is a refuge for us.

In this verse, *trust* is used as an imperative action verb, which means it is a command, not a suggestion. Trusting God "at all times" feels like a pretty steep command to me, almost unattainable, don't you think? "At all times" includes when doctors say there's no hope of having children, when the bank serves you a repossession notice, or when a doctor tells you that your daughter has a 50 percent chance of dying on the operating table.

Part of me wishes the psalmist had added a caveat to the command: "I know life gets really difficult, so disregard 'at all times' when something really terrible happens. It's okay to stay stuck in fear then." That caveat, obviously, isn't there. So what is God really telling us here? Did the psalmist mishear Him when He instructed us to trust "at all times"? Was He setting the bar so high that if we shot and missed, we would at least be in the vicinity of trusting? Could this be tough love or some kind of test?

Or is it possible that "trust . . . at all times" points to something not seen on the surface?

The Hebrew word translated "trust" is *batach*, which can be defined as "to be confident."[4] In the English language *trust* means "reliance on the integrity, strength, ability, surety, etc., of a person or thing."[5]

So maybe what the Lord is telling us in this verse is to be confident in Him and to be sure and secure in His ability, to put our hope in Him.

How is that possible to do "at all times"? Let me tell you a story.

I met Casey when I was thirteen years old at a crawfish boil at Danny Palmore's house in Baton Rouge, Louisiana. When I saw him serving the volleyball across the field from where I stood, I knew I wanted to meet him. For the next four years, we got to know each other platonically. When he finally asked me out in our church parking lot, I said yes because thus far he had proven to have good character—plus, he had great hair. Time went on, our relationship grew, and he asked me to marry him. Saying yes to Casey's proposal was a no-brainer because as I got to know him through dating, I'd learned even more about the good man that he is.

We have been married now for a quarter of a century. If you told me that you saw Casey stealing a television at Walmart, I would say you'd lost your mind. I've slept next to the man for years. I can complete his sentences. I know his nuances. More than twenty-five years of close relationship with Casey has inspired absolute confidence in me that he would not steal a TV.

You can't put full confidence in

AUTHENTIC TRUST CAN ONLY DEVELOP THROUGH LEARNING THAT A PERSON'S CHARACTER IS TRUSTWORTHY.

someone you don't know. Authentic trust can only develop through learning that a person's character is trustworthy.

That's especially true of trust in God. It develops as we come to know Him and His character. Jesus Himself explained how we come to know Him and how this kind of trust develops:

> So you must remain in life-union with me, for I remain in life-union with you. For as a branch severed from the vine will not bear fruit, so your life will be fruitless unless you live your life intimately joined to mine. I am the sprouting vine and you're my branches. As you live in union with me as your source, fruitfulness will stream from within you—but when you live separated from me you are powerless.
>
> (John 15:4–5 TPT)

The branch is completely dependent on the vine for life. If it becomes detached from the vine, it will wither and die because it's been removed from its source of sustenance. Jesus calls us the branches and Himself the Vine. Intimate relationship with Jesus means we remain attached to Him and He is the Source of all that we need. We don't look to ourselves to fill our need but rely on the abundant supply flowing deep within the Vine. But when life is too hard to understand and too painful to bear, we may be tempted to look away from Jesus and try to draw strength from our own meager resources. It just doesn't work!

Sometimes I find myself looking inward instead of upward. Imagine the different outcome for Adam and Eve if they had resisted Satan and drawn closer to the Father for answers instead of relying on their own reasoning. Remaining in the Vine is not a onetime interaction with Jesus, but a constant conversation, a continuous posture of attachment made possible by the Holy Spirit working through our surrendered hearts. That's when we realize that the sustenance Jesus gives outweighs what we create on our own. He becomes life to our souls, water for thirst, food for our hearts, and air for breathing.

Could it be that God's command to trust Him at all times isn't a demand for perfection but a call for constant connection, getting to know Him more and more deeply? I think so. We're invited to know Him not in a way we might know our child's teacher, but the way we know our spouse or best friend—intimately, in close union, heart to heart. The kind of knowledge that comes from sharing each other's celebrations and heartaches and being aware of each other's dreams, fears, and joys.

I've known my friend Sandy for thirty years. She can tell if I'm anxious or having a bad day simply by the tone in my voice when I say hello. That kind of union with God breeds trust, even the blind kind. Even though we can't predict His decisions, we know the ins and outs of His nature. In the command to trust Him at all times lies God's desire to know and be known by His created.

Trusting God at all times is a command that can only be obeyed through a deep, close, connected relationship in which He is our Source. And isn't that just like Jesus? To bypass rules and formulas and bring trusting Him through every nuance of life back down to the simplicity of relationship? In this safe space is where we experience a revelation of His love, power, and good character, which in turn inspires trust.

It becomes a cycle on repeat. Looking to Jesus as my Source produces intimacy. Intimacy produces trust. Trusting Jesus makes Him my Source, which produces intimacy, which produces trust. This cycle of trust and intimacy is what can settle the heart during a dark night of the soul, when we are faced with a crossroads of decision to trust Him or to crumble in fear and hopelessness. Attachment to Jesus is the hinge on which the door of trust hangs. We will walk through dark and dangerous valleys in life, but trusting Him is possible when we are connected to Him as our Source.

ATTACHMENT TO JESUS IS THE HINGE ON WHICH THE DOOR OF TRUST HANGS.

My attic door has a tendency to sag. When it does, it makes an awful screeching noise like nails on a chalkboard. Periodically my husband has to tighten the hinges to get it working properly. I've come to recognize that when I find myself anxious and stressed, I need to tighten the hinges in my relationship with God. Almost 100 percent of the time, I've allowed busyness to take over my life and pull me away from time with Jesus.

POWER AND POSSIBILITY

After that grueling consultation with the neurosurgeon, I decided I couldn't afford to camp out in Harran. Casey suggested that we scatter Haven's MRI scans on the floor, turn on worship music, and spend some time focusing our eyes on Jesus. We had to leave our natural ways of thinking behind and look to the Vine for sustenance, go to His table to find a supernatural way of thinking. I needed to see my situation from the perspective of His ability, from the eyes of possibility. I needed to filter the facts through Jesus' power.

My friend Stephen Chandler nailed the issue when he preached at our church and said, "Faith may not be your problem; awareness of God's power is the problem. Faith is the anchor, but it must be connected to the awareness of Jesus' power." Following Jesus takes us to the fertile land of possibility, where anything can be changed, resurrected, and healed. Endless possibility is a reality in God's kingdom. I needed reminding that there was a loving higher power at work doing what I couldn't do and that even the hell we were facing—this tumor and those awful statistics—was no match for Him.

Each black-and-white scan pictured an unmistakable large white mass trespassing in the back of Haven's skull. So here's what we did: We declared our trust in the Lord. We worshiped, prayed, confessed our belief in healing, and intentionally walked on top of those scans, symbolically putting Satan and his plans under our feet.

Fear did not bow easily. *I'm unbeatable*, it taunted. But every step I took on those slides was me answering back, *No, you're not!*

When we choose to follow Christ, all hell panics, because Satan gets a glimpse that what he sent to destroy us is actually serving to draw us closer to God. Hell's fury is no match for our obedience. Pain's agony is no match for God's power. As I paced the hospital floor, worshiping Jesus, my language changed from *God, please help me* to *God, I thank You that You are helping me! I see You in the middle of all this. You've already overcome this crisis; now help me to walk in Your victory!* This was a defining moment for me. I was learning to turn my tendency to panic into an opportunity to depend on God's wisdom, ability, and authority. Through worship our need became a sanctuary, a sacred womb growing our God awareness, a holy place where His presence touched the earth and brought peace and empowerment to my soul. Trust is God's answer to every challenge, heartache, and disappointment.

> **HELL'S FURY IS NO MATCH FOR OUR OBEDIENCE. PAIN'S AGONY IS NO MATCH FOR GOD'S POWER.**

HE IS TRUSTWORTHY

During a family vacation in the Caribbean a few years back, Casey and I allowed our kids to parasail. As each one rose above the ocean in a harness fastened to a giant parachute, attached to a contraption on a boat, we celebrated by cheering and taking pictures with our iPhones. But later that day, after all the excitement subsided, I started thinking about all that could have gone wrong.

First of all, the boat that held on to the parachute looked old and rickety. The seats were ripped, and the paint was rusting. Then I started thinking of how we'd trusted the parasailing company to have passed the standards that their country may or may not have standardized and enforced. What in the world was I thinking, entrusting my kids' lives to a company I knew so little about?

If you think about it, sometimes we have more trust in that which has a great risk of failure than in the God who literally spoke the world into being.

Think about what it takes for a human being to walk. The brain and spinal cord must be functioning together and properly. Then we take a step, and the real miracle begins:

> The centre of gravity . . . rises and falls and shifts from side to side. The arms swing, and the trunk rotates. The pelvis moves forwards on the side of the swinging leg, while the [opposite] shoulder does the reverse, keeping the head and eyes facing towards the direction for walking.[6]

While all this might seem second nature once we've learned to do it, it's actually quite complicated. And this intricate experience is possible not because two random mysterious stars collided, but because a wise Creator designed it.

The way a planted seed breaks apart and grows into a tree that produces food with the vitamins to sustain life, the way a baby is meticulously formed in the womb, the way the sun warms the earth each day from just the right distance—too close and we'd burn to death, too far and we'd freeze—all this is a miracle accomplished by Someone far more intelligent than we. We trust Him to keep the planets aligned, and we don't give a second thought to the sun rising every morning. We know it will appear over the eastern horizon because God in His wisdom says so. How much more can we trust His will for our lives?

I'm not trying to simplify life, because nothing about life is simple. It is complex and messy, but let's not be mistaken; it's not too messy for God. He isn't afraid to get His hands dirty. After all, He chose dust to make us from. May that be our reminder of just how small we actually are, but also of how God loves to engage in our mess.

What I do want to do is simplify our response to God. In the tension of what we don't understand, there is room for human emotion. We can get angry, disappointed, confused, and frustrated, but may we settle on choosing to trust. It's the only way to move forward to see God make a miracle out of the messes of life.

THREE

STAY THE COURSE

*Don't ask God to guide your steps if
you're not willing to move your feet.*
Unknown

I can almost see Terah meticulously studying his well-worn map, charting his course to Canaan. If he was like most of the males I know, he chose the fastest, most efficient route, and he probably lectured his grandkids beforehand about limited bathroom breaks. There was no way he was going to let a caravan he already passed get ahead of him because his group couldn't hold their bladders.

I imagine he set out on his journey with energy and enthusiasm from the thought of new possibilities. He was a nomad, ready to leave Ur in the background and move forward to something fresh. A dream was stirring within, a vision of the new land and the new life up ahead.

I remember back when Casey and I started Keypoint Church in northwest Arkansas, where we now pastor. In those early days we only knew one person in the area, but we had a ton of faith and excitement that God was going to build a church to reach people there. And He did. That first year at Keypoint was like a honeymoon. All the hard work was overshadowed by the newness. But eventually, of course, the newness began to fade. Reality hit. Obstacles came. And we had to learn perseverance and determination to continue what God had called us to.

This is hardly unusual. Whether it's when we first give our hearts to Christ, when God puts a dream inside us, or when a relationship begins, we usually start a new venture with hope and expectancy, but then the obstacles we encounter along the way conspire to slow us down. They may be intimidating, painful, confusing, or all three. We're disappointed—and understandably so. We expected that our relationship with God would be easier. We thought the dream would have materialized by now. We weren't supposed to be this wounded. So instead of pushing through and continuing to follow Jesus forward, too often we get stuck in what we can't figure out, disillusioned by the pain we didn't foresee, no longer sure if we want to trust God with our future.

Over the years of talking with so many people about their spiritual lives, I've seen this pattern emerge many times. Disappointment is birthed from unmet expectations. Staying the course means to stay *on course*, not straying left or right, not slowing down and not stopping.

Chances are, if we don't learn how to deal with our disappointment, we'll end up dying in Harran instead of reaching the promise God has in store for us. By "promise" I mean the fullness of His plans for our lives.

Obedience Changes Everything

The choice Casey and I made to uproot ourselves from Baton Rouge and move to Arkansas to start a church changed the trajectory of our family. Two of Haven's younger siblings were born in Arkansas. They have never known life in Louisiana. Their future, including who they meet and possibly marry, will result in part from that one decision we made.

Our choices, in other words, determine not only our future but the futures of those around us, although we often have no idea how impactful the steps we take today will be for our tomorrow. That was true for Terah as well. He had no idea that the journey he began would also bring his eldest son, Abraham, halfway to his promise. And the same journey that Terah stopped, stopped Abraham too.

Even though we don't know what lies ahead for us, we can be certain that God directs the scripts of the lives of those submitted to Him. So we can follow confidently in His steps—even when they lead us into difficult and confusing places or when we can't see the full picture—because we trust His path will end in a better place spiritually than where we currently stand.

Abraham couldn't have known just how significant the calling God placed on his life would be, but he was about to get a glimpse. While still living in Mesopotamia, before Terah moved the family to Harran, Abraham had heard God calling him (Acts 7:1–4). And then, after his father died in Harran, Abraham had his second God encounter.

> The LORD had said to Abram, "Go from your country, your people and your father's household to the land I will show you.
>
> > "I will make you into a great nation,
> >   and I will bless you;
> > I will make your name great,
> >   and you will be a blessing.

> I will bless those who bless you,
>> and whoever curses you I will curse;
> and all peoples on earth
>> will be blessed through you."

So Abram went, as the LORD had told him . . .

(Gen. 12:1–4)

A seed of great potential was buried inside Abraham, but its materialization was contingent upon his obedience.

For years I had a desire to host an annual women's conference for our church. But I'm not going to lie: I was scared. Scared no one would come. Scared I couldn't pull it off well and it would be a total flop. So I did nothing about my desire. I sat idle in my fear. For years. Waiting on a confirmation from God that He would make it successful. That confirmation never came, but one day my mindset changed. I felt the Lord speak. *Your indecision is from fear of being disappointed, but if you don't move forward, you and those you lead will miss what I have prepared.* Agreeing with that revelation put me in motion. We hosted our first conference and nearly one thousand women came. That taught me a great lesson: I have the power to stall God's plans for my life.

The Lord gave Abraham only one command: "Go." Then, six times after that, the Lord said, "I will . . ." followed by a specific promise. The condition was clear: *If you go . . . then I will do these things.* God hadn't yet fulfilled those promises—the nation inside Abraham was only a seed— but if Abraham stayed the course, he would walk right into his destiny.

Remember, Terah didn't set out to move *to* Harran, but to move *through* Harran to get to Canaan. The same was true for Abraham. But while the city became his father's dead end, it didn't have to be his own. Unknowingly, Terah had fulfilled God's purposes by bringing Abraham halfway to his promised destination, but the rest of the journey was up to Abraham. It was his choice to stay or go. And three words in verse 4 say all we need to know on how to stay the course in life: "So Abram went."

We are all works in progress, with buried seeds of potential. That means we don't have to have it all figured out right now. The potential inside us will grow into the harvest God ordained if we say yes when He says go. Even if you've lagged behind out of fear or disappointment, you can change that right now by saying yes to God.

Empowering Grace

"She will live because God is faithful." I said those words continually under my breath on the day of Haven's brain surgery.

An entourage of surgeons and nurses wearing their sterile garb met us in the surgery holding area. They were ready to take my daughter back to the operating room. For days I had dreaded this moment. Part of me had even expected God to prevent it from coming. The morning before, we had asked for another MRI to confirm the tumor was still there.

I'm sure the doctors questioned our sanity, but they had kindly appeased us. The tumor still existed. God had not yet worked a miracle, and now was the time to hand her over. I had to let her go.

It was like peeling off a layer of skin. I watched Haven reach out her hands and cry for me all the way down the hall. Eleven months old, with no idea why she felt bad, and strange people were taking her away from her mother. Excruciating.

The team turned the corner, and then they were gone. Salty tears and breathlessness ensued as Casey embraced me and we prayed. *Stay the course*, God whispered. *No matter what you hear or see, keep your faith in Me.*

The doctors had said the surgery would take eight hours and they would call every hour with an update. We went back to our room to wait. About thirty family members and friends were there to support us. Everyone congregated near me to offer encouragement, but I felt the pressing need to be alone. I needed just thirty minutes of real talk with God to get my thoughts straight.

I figured no one could follow me into our bathroom, so I ran water in the stand-up shower, undressed, and got in. Maybe the beating water pouring over my body would wash away my internal pain.

Several minutes ticked by and the tears came, at first like a trickle and then like a flood. Sinking to the shower floor, I wept and prayed and wept and prayed some more, my internal angst releasing through salty tears that fell from my eyes and trailed to the shower drain. It was cleansing. Holy. Grace met me there. God put His hands on my face, looked me in the eye, and said, *Trust Me. I've got this.*

I felt confidence in His words and nodded my head as if in agreement, choosing to believe that Haven not only would survive but would do well during the surgery. I breathed in the steamy air and focused on this peace, noticing my racing thoughts calming, my heartbeat slowing, and my body relaxing. Nothing had changed, and yet everything had changed. My spirit shifted from insecurity to confidence that Haven would live and I would be able to endure this. What happened in that shower was empowerment from grace. As Paul described in 2 Corinthians 12:9–10, grace can give us strength to do what we cannot do for ourselves:

> But he said to me, "My grace is sufficient for you, for my power is made perfect in weakness." Therefore I will boast all the more gladly about my weaknesses, so that Christ's power may rest on me. . . . For when I am weak, then I am strong.

That was my experience the day of Haven's first surgery. God satisfied my weakness with His perfect strength when I made a way to meet with Him, open my heart in honesty and transparency, and receive the transfer by taking God at His word.

Just one word from God, one encounter with His presence, can alter us if we receive it with faith. Abraham picked up all he owned and walked out of Harran because he had met with God and heeded His word. And I walked out of that bathroom a different person. I was able to genuinely smile, laugh with everyone, and hold meaningful conversations.

WHEN WE CAN'T, GOD CAN.

God's grace is a divine gift from the Father's hand for the purpose of empowering us, His children, to live out our days in victory. Real victory. When we can't continue, God will give us strength. When we can't see the way forward, God sees for us. When we can't, God can.

A LINE IN THE SAND

Haven's surgery lasted eight hours, just as the doctors said it would, and it went well. The surgeons used words like "remarkable" and "better than expected" to describe how she had fared. I was relieved to hear this news, but honestly none of this came as a surprise to me because of my encounter with grace in the shower.

We were anxious to see Haven in the ICU. For me, one question dominated all others: did she have posterior fossa syndrome, as the surgeon said she likely would? If so, she may not remember me or Casey and would probably be inconsolable. At the entrance to intensive care, we followed hospital instructions and scrubbed our hands and arms vigorously with disinfectant soap to get rid of any possible germs. Watching the orange liquid turn to foam on my limbs, I asked God to prepare me for this first time seeing Haven fresh out of brain surgery.

Her eyes were closed as we approached the bed, and I noticed that her thick brown hair had been shaved except for a tiny patch of bangs in the front. (How thoughtful of the doctors to consider that a momma might not yet be emotionally ready to let go of such a simple thing as hair.) I noticed the substantial swelling in her head and the large incision that ran from the middle of her head to the base of her neck. Tubes protruded from nearly every possible place on her body, attaching her to beeping and blinking machines.

My daughter's appearance was alarming, but she was alive and breathing, and that was enough for now. Gently I put my hand on her arm. "Haven," I whispered, "can you hear me?" This was the moment we had nervously anticipated. Casey, the social worker, the ICU nurse, and I all leaned in and held our breath to see what would happen next.

Haven had a thing she used to do called sweet eyes. She would squeeze her eyes shut in sort of a long blink. We had laughed the first time she did it, which of course made it stick, and it kind of became her thing. We would say, "Haven, give us sweet eyes," and on cue she would start blinking.

The next moment after I said her name, Haven made no sound, but squeezed her eyes tight in sweet eyes. It was her way of communicating to us. In an exhale of relief, tears trailed down all four of our faces. There was no sign of the syndrome. It was a miracle. She was in her right mind just an hour after major brain surgery. God answered this prayer, and that gave me faith to believe for the rest.

But the pendulum of life swings in extremes sometimes, doesn't it? One moment you're shouting "Amen" and the next you're crying "God help me!" Following Jesus is an upward progression, but that doesn't mean it's always linear. There will be bends and spirals and tests you thought you'd already passed. What you once thought was fixed for good might raise its ugly head again. Which is what happened to me the following morning, when we were informed that Haven would need another brain surgery.

After a follow-up MRI, the surgeon noticed a small piece of the tumor about the size of my thumb that he hadn't noticed during the initial operation. He said it had to be removed; there was no other option. If it was left behind, it would grow rapidly, so surgery was scheduled for the next morning. Then the litany of statistics began again, with a fifty-fifty chance she wouldn't survive the repeated surgery.

I have to do this all over again? I cannot fight yesterday's battle again tomorrow! And yet I heard the same confidence from the Lord: *I am the same yesterday, today, and forever. I have not left My post—don't leave yours. Stay the course.*

The words of Jeremiah 5:22 came to life in my heart and awakened my awareness of the power of God:

> "I made the sand a boundary for the sea,
>   an everlasting barrier it cannot cross.
> The waves may roll, but they cannot prevail;
>   they may roar, but they cannot cross it."

We are all familiar with the rolling and roaring of struggle. But we may forget that our trials and adversity have a stopping place. The blood of Jesus drew a line in the sand, limiting its reach. No matter how strong they roll and how loud they roar, remember we serve the God who controls the waves with His voice and has marked out a designated place they cannot cross. I took this promise to heart, that if God carried us through the first surgery, He could do it again. And

He did. Haven came out of the second operation the same as before, alive and with no posterior fossa syndrome.

By the end of our three-week stay at Le Bonheur Children's Hospital, we had turned a corner. Haven had defied every single statistic the surgeon had warned us of the first night. (With the exception of walking. She had just turned one and had not yet learned how.) We even had a chant—"We're getting out of here with a shout instead of a shunt"—to remind us of how good God had been. The pendulum had swung in our favor, and it seemed that every one of our prayers was being answered.

From the beginning, doctors had told us Haven's tumor was likely malignant, considering its large size and rapid growth. After her brain surgery, parts of the tumor were sent to pathology, and soon we would get the results. Daily I pushed the anxiety of waiting to the back of my mind and focused on the miracles I saw in front of me. Haven was alive! She had done so well in the surgeries. I told myself she was going to be okay. We were going to be okay. There was no sign of the dreaded posterior fossa syndrome.

If the tumor was benign, we could go home and resume life. There would be lots of physical and occupational therapy for Haven in her future and some hurdles she would have to overcome, but none of that mattered to me as long as we received a cancer-free diagnosis. My mind was set on packing my bags because surely we could keep riding this wave of answered prayer and would soon be headed home.

NOT WHAT I EXPECTED

"I'm going to dance with Haven at her wedding." It was a bold statement. The middle-aged pediatric oncologist from St. Jude Children's Research Hospital spoke it with persuasive confidence.

And we would need it because he had just told us Haven's tumor was malignant.

Cancer. No one wants to hear that word, especially related to a child. But there I sat, staring in the face of the doctor who said Haven was now accepted as a St. Jude patient. This was not the news we had hoped for. I was grateful Haven would get world-class care right there in Memphis, but a cancer diagnosis made our situation a thousand times more critical. This was no longer a recovery mission, but a beat-an-aggressive-cancer-to-survive mission.

The oncologist went on to explain Haven's chemotherapy protocol in detail—how many times a week she would receive it, the risks and side effects involved. Keep in mind that St. Jude is a research hospital, so Haven would be one of only seven children in the world receiving a new but promising experimental treatment. The course of this treatment would span a year, which meant that our new baby, just about eight weeks away from her due date, would be born in Memphis.

The prospect was daunting, and I couldn't help but question why. Why, when I was seeing so many miracles, couldn't God just do one more? Especially this one. God could have snapped His fingers and made all of this go away. But He chose not to, and that confused me. With Haven's recovery progressing so quickly, I was beginning to see the end of this ordeal. God was defying our odds, and I thought for sure He would defy this one too. Instead, He kept us on this course.

The idea of following Jesus on a dark path is frightening, especially when the ground beneath us gives way and the hands that hold us are the same hands that allowed it to quake. Yes, we have the assurance that He will lead us to victory if we keep in step with Him, even though the course may sway and buckle and turn and bend. But holding on to that assurance while we walk that path can sometimes take everything we've got.

I've learned that Satan senses the call on our lives and the potential inside us. We are a threat to his kingdom, and he will do whatever necessary to get us to stray off course or stop moving altogether. He knows that a detour will affect our lives' trajectory and has a trickle-down effect on our families and those we lead. So he crafts adversity that will cut to our quick and tells us it will never end. And then we struggle, not because we're weak or frail or God is unhappy with us, but because Satan understands what he's up against.

Our identity is "child of God." Our power is the demise of the enemy. Our promise is an eternal inheritance. Which is why enduring to the end is worth the cost. May we not forget the power of our calling, lest we be surprised by adversity. We struggle partly because we are doing something right.

Four Walls and Rotavirus

About a month after Haven became a patient at St. Jude and started chemotherapy, she contracted rotavirus. It's a common illness in young children and normally not that serious—unless you're in a hospital where other patients are critically ill with suppressed immune systems. In that case, a child with rotavirus gets placed in isolation.

If you're thinking of an isolation ward as a prison cell, you're not far off. It's a normal hospital room, but it's quarantined behind two separate sets of electronic doors. The protocol in isolation is that the patient cannot leave the room until he or she is no longer contagious. Nurses and doctors must wear sanitized gloves, hats, shoes, and smocks when they enter, and anyone entering and exiting the room must wash thoroughly. So this roughly twelve-by-twelve-foot space became our prison for the ten days it took for Haven to get over the virus.

Casey and I and our mothers, who had been visiting us on

alternating weeks, created a system so none of us would burn out emotionally during this time. We would take turns staying overnight with Haven in isolation so the others could rest in the hotel. When my time came to spend the night at the hospital, I thought for sure that being more than eight months pregnant I would get the sympathy vote. They wouldn't expect me to sleep on the uncomfortable couch-bed in that room, would they? But being at their wits' end, sympathy was vetoed, and I had to pull my own weight.

Let me set the scene for you.

Across from our room was another child in isolation behind another set of electric doors. I never laid eyes on this child or the family—in fact, I don't even know if it was a girl or boy—but I heard the child crying every other minute for ten days straight. Quite literally, the child never stopped. His or her parents must have been near mental breakdown, because I was close to losing my mind simply by proximity.

Haven wasn't allowed to leave her room, ever. I couldn't leave her alone, so I couldn't go anywhere either. Four peach-painted walls started closing in on me after only about an hour. With chattering cartoons repeating on our television and my unhappy one-year-old getting restless because her only option was to sit in a metal crib or on my lap, there was only so much a pregnant woman could stand.

My joints had already started to rebel at the stiffness of the make-shift bed, not to mention the sound of my skin peeling off the tacky pleather every time I moved. I couldn't even leave to get a snack, for crying out loud. What if I got a midnight craving?

Animated voices from our TV competed with the screams of the child next door. Haven let out her own cries of frustration as I sat on the couch, trying to will the child I carried within me to stop wrestling with my bladder. During my first night in isolation, all of this banded together and incited a coup that nearly overthrew me. With nowhere for my pent-up anguish to go, I released it by banging my head in rhythm on the wall behind me.

This must be what it feels like to go crazy. Wait! Am I going crazy? It feels like it. Why, God, won't You just make the child next door stop crying? Better yet, why not prevent rotavirus in the first place? Did we really need more complication? God, please, please, please get me out of here. Please? I repeated my desperate prayers over and over until I finally realized I wasn't going anywhere. Nothing was going to swoop down and rescue me from this night. I couldn't leave, and I had to face that fact.

I kept waiting for the familiar feeling of strength to infuse my soul and give me a new outlook. It never came. Every minute was grueling, as if the flesh of my will were being removed, layer by layer without anesthesia. It didn't feel fair. I begged for rescue, but I remained confined to that twelve-by-twelve room. Keep in mind, in that room I had everything I needed. Oxygen, food, a restroom, the luxury of air-conditioning, even a TV. Too often we blame outward circumstances for our inner issues. Isolation was isolating the desire within me to run from pain instead of build endurance in the midst of it.

Being in isolation never got easier, at least for me. Every shift I took in that prison was agonizing, and God in His wisdom chose not to rescue me. But here's the beauty in it all. Excruciating as it was, isolation became a tool for my good, showing me that though God doesn't remove every painful situation, He does endure it alongside me. And in the process, He builds the endurance I need to stay the course.

KEEP SWIMMING!

When I was in high school, I had a near-drowning experience in Cancún, Mexico. While enjoying the Caribbean water, I was suddenly caught in a riptide. I fought with all my might but nothing I did worked, and I panicked. I thought for sure I was going to meet a watery grave. Then, seemingly out of nowhere, a lifeguard appeared at my side. He held a float in one hand and my arm with the other. After we fought the current and the waves for what felt like ten minutes, he skillfully managed to navigate us out of the riptide and onto the shore.

The man saved my life. But I had to keep swimming while he did it.

I've come to believe as conviction that God always saves but doesn't always rescue in the way we think He should. Sometimes He's the Coast Guard jumping from the helicopter into rough seas. But more often He's the lifeguard who holds our arm, travails through the waves, and brings us to safety. If we keep our eyes on the shore, endure, and keep swimming, He'll get us there.

GOD ALWAYS SAVES BUT DOESN'T ALWAYS RESCUE IN THE WAY WE THINK HE SHOULD.

I didn't feel a miracle happening while in isolation, but that doesn't mean one wasn't taking place. His invisible, saving hand was steady. In fact, He used the weakness I was feeling to show me something about His power. Feeling His strength is not a requirement to operate in God's strength. Sometimes our senses are so fixed on our pain that our awareness of His abiding presence is pushed to the periphery. But that doesn't make His presence less real or less powerful.

We don't have to feel strong to be strong. We just have to keep walking (or crawling, if necessary) in the direction of God's leading and trust the Holy Spirit for the ability to continue on. In the end we'll find we are safe and secure. But we still have to endure.

Looking back to those excruciating nights in isolation, I see how God let me stay in that peach-colored prison to stretch and strengthen my mental, emotional, and spiritual endurance and to build my confidence that I can do hard things. The words of James 1:2–4 (TPT) took on new meaning as I realized how God had used adversity for my growth and empowerment:

> My fellow believers, when it seems as though you are facing nothing but difficulties see it as an invaluable opportunity to experience the greatest joy that you can! For you know that when your faith is tested it stirs up power within you to endure all things. And then as your endurance grows even stronger it will release perfection into every part of your being until there is nothing missing and nothing lacking.

It's not only in hard times like chemotherapy treatments and isolation stays that we'll need endurance, of course. We also need strength for the ordinary daily grind. To stay committed to exercising. To walk into the boardroom with a good attitude. To get up morning after morning and fix our child's peanut butter and jelly sandwich for lunch. Maybe we're discouraged and disappointed because we expected life to be different, more fulfilling, maybe more exciting. But it's not, and every day feels the same as we sit behind a desk or change the twentieth diaper. We thought we'd be married, out of debt, or two jean sizes smaller by now—and what happened to all the travel we planned when we were younger? Our vacations spent in the white villas nestled in the hills of Santorini are long-forgotten dreams because all our resources are spent keeping our bank account out of the red. The farthest we seem to get these days is the grocery store. Life feels ordinary, sometimes even draining.

That kind of everyday stress is particularly challenging for me because my personality thrives on change. I don't like to stay in one place for too long. I love to buy and flip houses. Big projects give me purpose, and I love variety. But God is helping me see that ordinary days, which make up the majority of my life, can become extraordinary if I see them as a piece of God's grander puzzle. He uses every hour, day, week, month, season, and year to transform me into the woman I'm called to be.

God works not only through the taxing days that rage like an angry river but also through the ordinary ones that flow by slowly like a lazy current. It's all part of God's broader plan for humanity, which is part of His vision for eternity. Guided by providence, both our dramatic and our ordinary days move us toward our destiny. But we must stay the course to cross the finish line, remembering that the same hand that upholds us in pain guides us in the mundane.

God's plans are generational, remember. We don't know how our legacy will extend into the future. But what we do with our days here and now reaches beyond us and affects more people than we realize. This is why God's work in our lives rarely features quick fixes, instant gratification, or short-term solutions. It's designed to produce what's best in the grand scheme of things, not only for us and those around us but for His kingdom at large.

Walking God's path for our lives takes spiritual muscle and internal grit, so we will need to develop these things in order to do it. And adversity is often the medium God allows and uses for our development. Like weight training to build great shoulders and biceps—for which I strive but still do not have—our struggles strengthen us by pushing us beyond what we think we can do. We can endure isolation. We can get out of debt. We can survive our unwanted divorce. We can. When we draw from our Source for endurance and press on even when it hurts, the problems that were sent from our enemy to destroy us actually make us stronger. Resolving to stay the course when we want to quit builds backbone and creates the kind of tenacious endurance that only comes from adversity.

No Quick Fixes

I've had several spinal injections of cortisone to relieve pain in my upper neck caused by a bulging disk. While cortisone can be a source of instant pain relief, it can also make matters worse if overused.

The same is true of quick fixes in the spiritual lessons God is teaching me. Honestly, when I'm looking to satisfy my desire for pain relief in my soul, what I really want is something to make me feel better right now. I want to be rescued regardless of whether I interrupt the process of building character, bringing me closer to God, and setting up my future for success. All I can see is that I'm hurting and I want the pain to stop, even if it means giving up or ignoring God's call. But that kind of quick fix is like too much cortisone. It will weaken us spiritually.

Here's another way to look at it. Pain is the playground bully that forces us to reroute our path to avoid a confrontation. But I'm learning not to let my discomfort bully me into missing what endurance produces in my soul. I don't want to trade eternal work for temporal relief.

What we often miss when we insist on quick fixes is that we may be creating more pain and regret because we are forfeiting the layers of strength and endurance that staying the course builds. With this added strength we can break through barriers and go to new levels to see more of our dreams fulfilled.

In saying all this, I don't want to trivialize what you may have been through or order you to "just toughen up." I simply want to encourage you that building endurance is worth it. So that instead of retreating when obstacles seem insurmountable, you'll consider that the obstacles can be dealt with one step at a time. Because progress is far more important than perfection.

The race isn't complete until you cross the finish line, but it will never be complete if you don't keep running. What the other person did is too hard to forgive . . . until you try (and try again). A child fighting cancer is too difficult to endure . . . until you take it one day at a time. God didn't ask me to endure the year; He asked me to give Him each day.

Let's not be people who shrink back or give up because we can't make sense of God's ways or don't feel His presence in the moment. He's with us always. He's using whatever we experience to build our character, strengthen our spiritual backbone, and further His kingdom.

I wonder how many miracles have never materialized because we abandoned our posts and strayed off course. I wonder how many destinies are on pause. Let's be those people who stay the course so the generations after us have a better foundation to walk on.

You are strong enough. Tenacious enough. Through the power of the Holy Spirit within you, you have what it takes.

So, pack your bags. We're moving on.

FOUR

THE OUTLINE OF HIS PRESENCE

Several weeks after Haven started chemotherapy treatments, her oncologist approached us with a favor to ask. CBS News wanted to interview Casey and me to shed light on Haven's new, groundbreaking chemotherapy treatment. Her doctor all but begged us to say yes. He said it would bring national attention to this experimental treatment, which could help other children suffering with brain cancer. Reluctantly we agreed.

A few short days later, camera crews arrived in Memphis to film a day in our lives. They showed up at our hotel room early that morning with cameras and followed us everywhere from the hospital cafeteria—seriously, why would anyone be interested in watching us eat lunch?—to the room where Haven was undergoing treatment. Toward the end of the day, Casey and I sat down for an interview.

They turned on the blinding lights, and the interviewer started asking questions like "How did you react when you found out Haven had brain cancer?" and "How are you coping with everything?" We did our best to give answers that were hopeful and God honoring, but honest.

I remember watching that segment on television early one morning not long afterward. I almost gasped when the reporter said things like "The long-term odds are against Haven, and there are no guarantees and many risks." I had heard this from her doctors, but seeing all this from an outside perspective made me realize anew just how critical our situation was. *Is this really my life?*

When the segment ended, an unexpected, heavy sadness settled in my heart. Unable to shake it, I went to the shower, my place of solitude, and sank to the floor. It seemed as though I had been meeting God there a lot lately. I had no words because I was struggling to dissect and label my emotions. Did I feel vulnerable, sorry for myself, angry, afraid, embarrassed? Maybe a mixture of all these. I offered God what I had: my sighs. And from the comfort that washed over me like the warm water beating down on my skin, I sensed that God heard every wordless breath.

Words aren't always necessary to articulate our longings to our heavenly Father because of the truth that He is close to us at all times, leaned into our hearts—I'm talking ear to the chest. Just as a loving mother can interpret her child's cries from the inflection in his voice, the Holy Spirit is so deeply involved in our lives that He interprets the cry of our hearts even in our sighs. That's what the psalmist meant when he wrote:

> You know what I long for, Lord;
> you hear my every sigh.
>
> (Ps. 38:9 NLT)

AM I ALL ALONE?

Have you ever heard of deism? It's a philosophy that first became popular hundreds of years ago. It basically holds that the Creator set the world in orbit and then walked away, distancing Himself from His creation to let it fend for itself. While deism does acknowledge a higher power, what good is a higher power that is uninvolved and disconnected from its creation? Deism is a crafty lie woven together by Satan in an effort to intercept our Source. Some people point to evil and chaos in the world as evidence that God doesn't care about us.

Nothing could be farther from the truth. And nothing could be more harmful, especially these days, when we need real connection more than ever.

There are more people on our planet today than ever before. Through the power of smartphones and the internet, we are afforded more options than ever to connect. The number of people on social media today—more than two billion—is astounding. Sadly, even with all this connection, people feel lonely and isolated. Pseudo relationships have replaced real ones; we are connecting screen-to-screen but not face-to-face. With so much power at our fingertips, our natural human longing to be seen, heard, known, and touched remains unfulfilled. Our longing cries out for an answer: *Does anyone hear me and see me, or am I all alone?*

Severe or prolonged pain can make the sense of isolation worse. We question, *Am I the only one feeling this way? Can anyone understand what I'm going through?* And scrolling through our friends' polished social media feeds sure makes it feel as though we're alone in the struggle.

When Haven was in chemotherapy at St. Jude, I was five hours away from family and friends—and this was in an era with no smartphones or FaceTime. Maybe that worked partly in my favor because at least there was no social media to give me FOMO[1] and cause me to compare my stressed life with the fun it looked like other people were having.

But the lack of social-media connection brought its own set of problems. Because we were out of sight and out of mind, everyone back home continued their regular lives without us. We'd get the occasional visitor (in addition to our moms), but for the most part we were on our own. And it was lonely. Often I felt isolated not just by lack of proximity but by my pain. Very few people could identify with my struggles, and that made it harder for me.

The few times we were able to go back to Baton Rouge for short visits, I still felt disconnected, almost as if life there were a spinning Ferris wheel, and I couldn't figure out where to jump on. To make things worse, I was riding a different Ferris wheel altogether—cancer and chemotherapy—and I couldn't figure out how to jump off. I needed to know that someone saw me and heard me—not just my situation, but me, what I was feeling and fearing. I needed to know that I wasn't alone. I wonder how frequently I've bought into subtle lies about God in my times of disappointment. Perhaps we gradually come to think that maybe, just maybe we're on our own because God didn't come through the way we thought He should have. It's easy to believe when our eyes are focused on our pain instead of searching for God's presence. And Satan uses this time to whisper artful lies into our vulnerable ears. But God is always whispering, too, and if we learn how to sense Him, we will see Him.

Saturating the Bible from start to finish are countless messages that God is not just near humanity, but deeply concerned and actively involved in it. The Bible itself, which contains the very words of God, is tangible proof that God wants to communicate with His children. He secured its existence through the millennia just so we would know His heart.

In the Old Testament, God revealed Himself countless times to His people. He was committed to walk with the nation of Israel and to be their guide. In the New Testament, God clothed His presence with flesh when Jesus was born on the earth. His name was Immanuel, which means "God with us." Can you imagine the moment Jesus let out His first lusty cry as a newborn? All of heaven must have been awestruck that the Creator wanted intimacy with His creation so much that He sent His Son to conquer hell to make it happen. Then after Jesus ascended to heaven, God sent the Holy Spirit, to live in the hearts of those submitted to Him. All for nearness. God goes to great lengths to make sure we know the kind of relationship He desires with us: up close and personal.

BECAUSE YOU ARE HIS

During one of Haven's hospital stays, she woke up in the middle of the night, tapping on my arm and asking to watch one of her favorite shows. She was tucked in close to my side because we were sharing the hospital bed. It was dark and late, and I was tired, but I grabbed the remote and turned on the television without a second thought. If she had asked for all the stars in the sky and they were within my power to give, I would have plucked them down one by one and handed them to her on a golden platter. She was my daughter, and for me there was hardly a greater joy than to meet her desires.

Identity and proximity are everything. We are not God's acquaintances; we are His children. We are tucked in close right next to Him. We already have His listening ear, and we can trust Him to delight in us and care for us.

One night, years later, as I sat in a movie theater with Casey on a date, I saw the screen of my silenced cell phone light up. It was the new babysitter calling me. She was watching our second daughter, Holland, who was born while we were in Memphis for Haven's treatment, and our younger sons, Hayes and Hudson. I picked up the phone and quietly whispered, "Hello."

I heard sniffing on the other end of the line and then, "I can't find Holland."

What does she mean she can't find Holland?

"Did you look in her room, the bathroom, in the backyard?"

"Yes," she said. "All the neighbors are out looking for her. We can't find her, and I'm about to call the police."

Never once in that conversation did the thought cross my mind, *You know, I have more than one kid. It would be nice not having to spend any more time correcting her, so no worries; call off the search.* Never. In fact, I bolted from my chair and ran out to the lobby, forgetting to tell Casey what was going on and about to race to my car. Then the thought hit me to ask the babysitter if she had looked in the game room. I called her and stayed on the line while the sitter walked to the game room and opened the door. There sat Holland, watching a movie, completely oblivious to the panic of half the neighborhood.

I'll never forget the wave of relief that swept over me in that moment. Because Holland is my child, no matter how much I have to correct her, no matter how often she tries my patience, no matter how many times she stomps away from our conversations, she's mine, and I fiercely love what's mine.

HIS LOVE AND APPROVAL AREN'T BASED ON WHAT WE DO, BUT WHO WE ARE: HIS CHILDREN.

The Bible makes it clear that God feels that way about each of us too. We are His children, so when we cry out to Him as "Abba, Father" (Mark 14:36), we don't have to raise our voices. The Holy Spirit is so close that He hears our whispers. And He's a good Father. There is no need to prove ourselves to Him because His love and approval aren't based on what we do, but who we are: His children.

There is no need to beg for His attention. We already have it. When we're overwhelmed, we don't even need words to articulate our needs to Him, because the Holy Spirit translates our sighs and groans and then meets those needs according to His will (Rom. 8:26–27).

NEVER, NEVER, NEVER

Because God loves us and because we are His children, He will never abandon us, no matter how our pain or other circumstances make us feel. Hebrews 13:5 spells it out for us:

> Never will I leave you;
> never will I forsake you.

We don't see it in our English versions, but in Greek, the original language of the New Testament, the writer used double negatives in this verse. If translated today, it would be something like, "I will not, not, not, no never forsake you." In high school I had a friend whose mom often used double negatives. One of her favorite sayings when we were stressed about an outcome was "You can't never tell." It was terrible grammar, but it stuck with me, and maybe that's why. Instead of two negatives nullifying each other, as they do in English, double negatives in ancient Greek give an intense negative emphasis.

As the great English preacher Charles Haddon Spurgeon put it,

> If God has said, "I will not, not, NOT, no never forsake my people," we must believe Him, and we must chase away all thought of the possibility of the Lord's forsaking His servants or leaving them to perish.[2]

Just in case we didn't get it the first time, God declares, again and again, five times, that He'll never leave us. No matter what we go through, abandonment by God will not, not, not, no never happen.

I've read heroic stories about Jewish mothers in the Holocaust that illustrate this point. When trains filled with Jewish captives arrived at concentration camps, the German soldiers would separate the people into two lines, one for the strong and the other for the weak, and the weak would be led to their deaths. It was said that soldiers would fight mothers to pry their children from their arms and place them in the line for the weak. But the mothers, knowing their children would be killed, wouldn't let go. Some even begged to go with the children because they could not bear the thought of them suffering alone.

Tired of fighting the mothers, the soldiers eventually conceded and often sent both mothers and children to the line to die. Even the threat of death couldn't separate a mother from her child. She would stay with her child to the bitter end.

What a vivid picture of the love God possesses for His children. His love is fierce and wild, like that of a mother who will protect her child from any threat at all costs, even if it means giving her own life.

I've never been through anything remotely close to the Holocaust, but I can certainly relate to those mommas. You can mess with me, but don't mess with my kids. My sweet Southern ways will take a quick turn, and momma bear will come out to greet you.

When my son Hayes was in kindergarten, a random teacher at the school accused him of lying about a piece of trash that wasn't his. Anyone who knows Hayes knows that this teacher was mistaken. It's not that it's impossible for him to lie, but he is conscientious by nature and, especially at five years of age, just thinking he might be in trouble would make him cry.

THE OUTLINE OF HIS PRESENCE | 67

Twice that day when the teacher saw Hayes in the hallway at school, she pointed her finger at him and said, "I know you lied!" That made Hayes burst into tears and hives. By the time he made it off the bus after school that day, he was spent. And just hearing what happened made smoke come out of my ears.

I've made a point not to raise snowflakes and to teach my kids to always respect authority, but I couldn't let Hayes suffer humiliation from this teacher by himself. I got into my car immediately, drove to the school, and let this teacher know in the sternest voice I could muster that she needed to back off.

God is a heavenly Parent who won't leave us to suffer pain alone. He vows to be with us until the end with a locked grip that won't be undone. Our pain can't hide us from His presence. If we run to God, in fact, He hides us *in* His presence.

How Do I Know He's Near?

I've come to believe that I'll never be able to fully grasp just how near God's presence is to me and, even more, why He would want to be so close. I would not be so presumptuous as to even begin to understand why God wants to know me so deeply. But He says He does in His Word, and I choose to believe it.

Sometimes that's a challenge for me, though, especially right in the middle of trials or unmet expectations or my own frustration when I don't see or feel Him. If He's near, where is the evidence? If He's watching and knows how much I hurt, why isn't He changing my situation? Is He still in control, or has He let go of the reins? He has the power to fix it, stop it, and change it, but it feels as if He's indifferent to my pain.

When I was about five years old, a neighbor dropped me off at home after school thinking my family was inside. But when I walked in the door, I realized I was alone. It was a simple miscommunication, and someone would be home soon, but at the time I didn't know that. I remember immediately panicking because it was now up to me to take care of myself. And I felt completely incapable. I wasn't big enough to fight off strangers, and I couldn't cook myself dinner. The world was too big for me to survive in it alone, and I knew it.

Deep down, even as grown-ups, we know that life is too big for us to handle alone. We weren't created to live outside of a relationship with Christ, so life without Him will always prove to be too much. If we don't understand that His abiding presence will never leave us, insecurity and fear will drive us. But when His constancy becomes our conviction—and I mean when we *really* believe it—life becomes less worrisome.

> **WE WEREN'T CREATED TO LIVE OUTSIDE OF A RELATIONSHIP WITH CHRIST, SO LIFE WITHOUT HIM WILL ALWAYS PROVE TO BE TOO MUCH.**

According to Psalm 139, there is nothing we can do that God doesn't already know. There is no place we can run or hide that He can't reach. There is no darkness that can hide us from His light. It's sobering to realize that God sees straight through us, but it is also comforting to know that we are loved by Someone who knows us through and through.

> You have searched me, LORD,
>   and you know me.
> You know when I sit and when I rise;
>   you perceive my thoughts from afar.

You discern my going out and my lying down;

>   you are familiar with all my ways.

Before a word is on my tongue

>   you, LORD, know it completely.

You hem me in behind and before,

>   and you lay your hand upon me.

Such knowledge is too wonderful for me,

>   too lofty for me to attain.

Where can I go from your Spirit?

>   Where can I flee from your presence?

If I go up to the heavens, you are there;

>   if I make my bed in the depths, you are there.

If I rise on the wings of the dawn,

>   if I settle on the far side of the sea,

even there your hand will guide me,

>   your right hand will hold me fast.

If I say, "Surely the darkness will hide me

>   and the light become night around me,"

even the darkness will not be dark to you;

>   the night will shine like the day,

>   for darkness is as light to you.

(Ps. 139:1–12)

Every minuscule detail about our lives is accounted for. Details stress me out. It's not my personality to focus on them. But God, He is into the details. This is why when life is worrisome and we don't know how things will work out, we can trust and leave the details up to Him. Through trials, we've got to be big-picture thinkers. The big picture is that the God who works all things for our good is always with us. It's His loving-kindness that compels Him to journey with us in the highs and lows, the days and nights, the sadness and celebrations of life, and to protect us from harm.

Scripture tells us (Ps. 28:7; 1 Peter 1:5; and many others) God's presence acts as our daily shield, which our enemy can't penetrate. He is with us, and because of His presence, we will not only survive but be victorious. Of course, those who reject God can conquer life's trials as well, but by victory I'm referring to triumphing over our enemy by winning the daily battles, bringing God glory, and having a greater revelation of Him.

I recently learned a new word. It's actually fairly old, used mainly in the early 1900s, and I think we need to bring it back into circulation. The word is *pluck*, and it means courage or resolution in the face of difficulties. I want more pluck. I want to be a plucky woman. Spiritual pluck isn't the absence of fear; it's choosing to trust God's loving-kindness in the face of fear, believing that He is actively being God of the details in our lives, working in ways we can't, knowing that we're never alone.

When God Is Hard to See

Not long ago we received a phone call one evening. A friend's son had committed suicide. Just a few weeks later, another phone call came, this time at four o'clock in the morning. A friend in our church had died in a car accident. Then just a few weeks after that, the call came at midday. A friend's husband had left her. It was like dominoes. The calls kept coming one after the other, and I was afraid of what the next call might be.

In times like that, when so many bad things happen at once, we may struggle to see evidence of God's hand or face—really any body part will do. We long to know that He's still close and in control. But sometimes, to be quite honest, He just seems to be . . . absent.

He's not, of course. His promise to never leave us will always hold. But what do we do when we just can't see Him or feel Him? How do we access the comfort we need?

First of all, we need to keep in mind that while He may not be visible and audible, God can always be seen and heard. God leaves trace evidence of Himself everywhere. We just have to look for it. And nothing makes us look for light more than darkness. But I've found that the darkness can be a great illuminator of God's light.

Jeremiah 29:13–14 promises, "You will seek me and find me when you seek me with all your heart. I will be found by you."

Seekers have privileges. They find Jesus.

What does it mean to seek Him? We can seek Him mainly through prayer, in the Word, through worship. But if a constant connection with God is our mindset and discipline, then we can make shopping at the grocery store or driving in our car opportunities to search for Him. Seeking God is a heart posture of desiring Him. May we be people who seek God and run to Him rather than worry, instead

SEEKERS HAVE PRIVILEGES. THEY FIND JESUS.

of relying on old habits, material things, and temporal enjoyment. Matthew 6:33 promises that when we do this, He'll take care of everything else we need. We can seek Him not just for pain relief or miracles, not just for quick fixes, but to engage with Him in conversation and relationship. We can seek Him to know Him as intimately as He knows us—impossible, of course, but at least we can try. Every layer He allows us to peel back is a privilege that only those who seek Him are rewarded.

God wants us to make searching for His heart a priority. But that doesn't mean God plays hard to get. No, He tells us to seek Him because He wants to be found.

Some versions of the Bible translate Jeremiah 29:14 as "I will let you find me" (NRSV). I love that wording because it reminds me of a loving parent playing hide-and-seek with a small child. Little ones are rarely efficient seekers, but parents make sure their search is rewarded. They'll hide in easy places or even stomp out to reveal themselves.

I believe God does that with us. Yes, He wants us to seek Him. But in His loving-kindness—and out of His great love—He not only lets us find Him but also actively reveals Himself to us.

HIS PRESENCE IN OUR MIDST

In the ten months we battled for Haven's life, we received very few reports that were positive and only seldom days were good. It would be easy for me to say that the year 1999 was nothing but horrific. But that wouldn't be entirely true. When the presence of God is with us, His goodness manifests all around us. And if we look for it, we will notice it in nearly everything from the air that we breathe to the rising of the sun. But sometimes God makes a dramatic spectacle of His presence just to be sure we see Him. That's what He did for me with a man on a plane. It happened the day we first flew to Memphis with Haven, two days after she was first diagnosed. On the plane from Baton Rouge, I noticed that the man sitting across the aisle from Casey glanced our way a few times. I assumed he was just inquisitive because my eyes were red-rimmed and teary and I wore a shell-shocked expression on my face that wasn't easily dismissed.

A few minutes into the flight, the man asked Casey why we were traveling to Memphis. Casey explained that our daughter had been diagnosed with a brain tumor and we were going there to meet with a neurosurgeon. The man reached into his suit jacket, pulled out a white envelope, and handed it to us. "I serve on a board for a nonprofit that financially helps families whose children are hospitalized, mainly with cancer, and I want you to have this check."

To this day I can't remember the man's name or the amount of the check. I only remember feeling the overwhelming sense that God was close. That encounter was like feeling His breath on my cheek. Through that interaction on the plane, God told me loud and clear, *Stacy, I hear you, I see you, and I will not, not, not, no never leave you. Just keep following Me.*

God reveals Himself in big and small ways that mark the outline of His presence in our midst. When I looked for Him, He let me find Him, sometimes in jaw-dropping, miraculous ways.

In the days after becoming patients at St. Jude, we lived in a hotel. The Ronald McDonald House affiliated with St. Jude was completely occupied, so the hospital provided us with two hotel rooms to stay in for the time being. Unfortunately the hotel was an older establishment with a dark, creepy parking garage and carpet so worn I couldn't tell the color beneath all the stains. I didn't feel I had the right to complain, but I also worried I wouldn't be able to care adequately for our soon-to-be newborn and a child undergoing chemotherapy in a room with two beds and a dorm-size refrigerator. But the time for our new daughter's arrival was not yet upon us, so I forced myself not to worry about it. I left mental space that perhaps something would work in our favor and a room at the Ronald McDonald House would come available.

One morning I stayed behind at the hotel while Casey and my mom took Haven for her daily appointment at the hospital clinic. I was sitting on the bathroom counter, straining toward the mirror so I could see to put on mascara under the dim hotel lights, when suddenly a thought hit me. *I would love to have an apartment here in Memphis—something like the Gates in Baton Rouge.* The Gates was a new, upscale gated apartment complex that I had driven by a few times recently. I hadn't been thinking about apartments; the thought just scrolled through my mind like ticker tape and then was gone. I never spoke it out loud. I never prayed it to the Lord. It was a simple fleeting thought of seemingly no consequence.

About an hour later the phone in my hotel room rang. I answered it and heard a man say, "You don't know me, but I am a friend of a friend. I heard about your situation, and I want to help you. I own some apartments in Memphis like the ones in Baton Rouge called the Gates. Are you familiar with those? Anyway, the complex is on a golf course, and I have a fully furnished apartment on the seventh-hole green that I'd like you to live in until you are released to move back home."

I hung up the phone in disbelief. *How? What? I don't understand . . .* Then the tears came. No one could have known my fleeting thought just an hour before. The topic had never come up in discussion between Casey and me. Only God knew because His ear is always on my heartbeat. And He illuminated His presence so I could remember that He's continually working behind the scenes in my daily life. He wanted to be found so that I would know I am never alone.

THE KALEIDOSCOPE

Our awareness of what God is doing in our lives doesn't change His involvement. He is with us whether we know it or not. But being aware of God's nearness *will* change our response to pain. Zephaniah

3:17 says that God is singing songs of joy over us. When heartache has extinguished the light from your heart, His song prophesies into the darkness that you are a loved child of God who will overcome. He is singing, speaking, and prophesying His will for us continually, but we must train our eyes and ears to see and hear the presence of God.

Sometimes I seek God's hand more for pain relief than I seek His face to know His heart. We won't find the fullness of God this way, only a one-dimensional picture that falls flat and dull until we seek Him to know Him deeply. But when we do seek His face and we become aware of His presence, the richness and beauty of what we discover will astonish us again and again.

Like a kaleidoscope that reveals new pattern and color with every turn, a search for God will reveal His multifaceted good nature, which never ceases to amaze. His presence is hidden in everything from great displays of victory to bottomless lows of defeat and everything in between. He shows us in tangible and intangible ways that He is near.

Look for Him at every angle and in every corner and you will find Him. If all you see is disappointment, keep turning the kaleidoscope. When you seek Him with all your heart, your place of discouragement can become the very place where you find God.

FIVE

JOY THAT HEALS

"Are you sure you'll be all right?"

"Absolutely, Mom. There's nothing to worry about."

My mother had been in Memphis with us for seven days and was scheduled to leave on a Wednesday night. Casey's mom and dad and sister were scheduled to arrive the next morning. That meant Casey and I would be alone with Haven for the night, and this was something new for us.

Since the beginning of Haven's treatment, our routine had been the same. Casey's mom and my mom would stay with us on alternating weeks—one mom arriving just as the other mom left. This would be the first time we would be without one of them, but we were feeling pretty confident.

Yes, Haven had received a chemotherapy treatment that day. And yes, I was nine months pregnant by now. But I had already decided this baby's birth would go calmly and smoothly. And surely things would go according to my plan. I was feeling pretty good, and Haven's treatments had become more or less routine for us. Besides, there would only be a few hours' gap; surely we could handle that. We said goodbye to my mom and assured her that we would see her in a week when Casey's mom left.

About three o'clock the following morning, I woke up with sharp labor pains. *You've got to be kidding me.*

Because of yesterday's chemotherapy, I decided to labor as long as I could at the apartment instead of dragging Haven to another hospital in the middle of the night. But after two hours the pains became stronger, so I woke up Casey and told him I needed to go to the hospital soon. Rubbing his eyes, he told me to get more sleep because it would probably be a few more hours.

Have I mentioned that my husband is *not* a doctor—and that he was *not* the one in labor? I should have thrown the car keys at him, but instead I considered that he was most likely right and took a bath. But after about an hour, I knew we couldn't wait any longer. I told him to get dressed because we were leaving soon.

I rushed to wake Haven. Then suddenly the pain got so intense that I feared the baby might be born in the apartment. I burst into the bedroom to find Casey casually shaving in front of the mirror. (Just once I'd love for a man to experience a labor pain.)

I don't know exactly what words I used, but Casey threw down his razor, grabbed Haven, and ran for the car. We rushed to the hospital, which was twenty-five minutes away. On the way there I felt the labor turn. Contractions became unbearable, and I started to panic. Casey's eyes grew as big as the moon when he realized that he might have to deliver this baby on the side of the road. Needless to say, he pushed down harder on the accelerator.

Finally, we careened up to the emergency room entrance and I was wheeled into labor and delivery. As Casey followed behind, he held Haven, who was crying in fear at seeing me in duress. We quickly realized Casey wouldn't be able to stay with me, so he paced the halls with Haven while I was in the delivery room.

It's okay, I told myself. *I can handle this.*

As I mentioned earlier, I'm not a fan of pain. Now I need to make it clear that I am *really* not a fan of pain, especially in childbirth. I consider the epidural one of the greatest inventions in human history. In fact, with my last two children I practically went into the hospital backward, pointing to where the doctor could put the needle. In my mind there's no need for senseless pain when some brilliant person invented a medicine that blocks it. I know all of you natural-childbirth believers are probably offended by me right now, but this girl will take all the meds they willingly give me.

I've never understood why someone would play down their pain. When the nurses show me the chart with the smiling and frowning faces and ask me to rate my pain on a scale from one to ten, I am going to point to the frowning face and say ten every time. Why would anyone say three? The way I look at it, it's the one time in my life I can get legal drugs on demand, so I'm taking advantage of it!

While I'm only *partly* joking, I think I've made my point that I didn't want a natural childbirth. But now the doctors were telling me that my labor was too far along for an epidural.

What? This was not in my plan! Not what I expected. I take it all back. This I cannot handle.

Hearing that news on top of our chaotic arrival made me tense up, which made the contractions stronger. I'm sure that my screams could be heard in the next county.

At that point the hospital chaplain entered the room. News had probably spread quickly about the crazy lady screaming in the delivery room. She walked over and said she'd heard that my husband couldn't be with me and asked if I wanted her to stay. At that point I didn't care if the president were in the room. I just wanted the whole thing to be over. In between pants and shrieks I told her she would have to stay at her own risk because I couldn't be held responsible for anything I said or did.

Thirty minutes later, our second daughter was born with dramatic flair—very fitting to her personality today. We named her Holland Grace to remind us of the grace God had showered on us during this season. Casey was finally able to come into the room with Haven to meet Holland, and once he realized that she and I were okay, a mischievous grin formed on his face. Every time I looked at him, he was wearing that darn smirk. Is it okay to tell you that I may have wanted to slap it off? I knew exactly what he was doing—teasing me for my insanity.

I called Casey's mom to see how far away she, his dad, and his sister were from Memphis. "About twenty minutes," she replied.

"Oh good," I told her. "Don't worry about going to the apartment because I'm at the hospital. You have a new granddaughter."

I could hear their car erupt in laughter over the phone. It was contagious, and I started laughing too.

Later in the day, the chaplain came to my room to formally introduce herself and tell me that witnessing Holland's birth had been the most beautiful experience of her life. How was any of my crazy beautiful? Mortified about my behavior, I begged her to forget anything I'd said or done and to try, if she could, to erase all the images out of her mind.

That night my sister-in-law stayed with me at the hospital. The room was quiet, and the lights were dim. Then suddenly a memory hit me, and I let out a hysterical laugh.

"What are you laughing at?" she asked.

"I just remembered something I did during labor. My mouth was dry because of all my screaming. I kept begging for water, but they would only give me a few ice chips. But someone put a wet rag on my forehead, so I grabbed the rag and started sucking the water from it. I am never showing my face to those people again!"

She and I laughed over that story for about thirty minutes because that kind of behavior—screaming, allowing a woman I'd never met to stay with me in delivery, and sucking on a towel—is so unlike me. I would end up skipping my six-week checkup because I was too embarrassed to face that doctor again.

There's hardly a year that goes by when someone doesn't bring up Holland's birth story at our family gatherings. My sister-in-law even framed a picture of me right after the birth with a look on my face that says, "Dear God, what in the world just happened?" She sets it out on the table just to get laughs. In fact, we're still laughing about the craziness of it all today. It was awful and hilarious at the same time. Finding the humor has helped me see the entire day as dramatic instead of traumatic.

Psychologist Tasha Eurich believes that looking for the humor in our difficult or painful circumstances can make all the difference in getting through them. For those who are experiencing stress, she tells us:

> Mark Twain said, "humor is tragedy plus time." So, when something stressful happens, ask, "Will I think any part of this is funny in a week or a month?" Give yourself permission to experience that reaction now.[1]

Nothing makes this statement truer to me than my memories of when Holland was born.

Joy Is Good for Us

Scientific studies have proven that joy is good for both our emotional and our physical health. Eurich explains how this works. "When we laugh, our bodies release endorphins and dopamine, nature's feel-good chemicals. The result? We can better cope with stress, find hope, and see problems in new ways."[2]

Researcher Courtney Ackerman expands on that idea by explaining:

> Positive emotions can actually act as a buffer between you and stressful events in your life, allowing you to cope more effectively and preserve your mental health. . . . In addition, in 2006 researchers confirmed that experiencing positive emotions helps you modulate your reaction to stress and allows you to recover from the negative effects of stress more quickly.[3]

Science proves what God's Word told us thousands of years ago, that internal joy is a healing agent for our bodies and souls:

> A joyful, cheerful heart brings healing to both body and soul.
> But the one whose heart is crushed
> struggles with sickness and depression.
>
> (Prov. 17:22 TPT)

It's clear that joy is essential to being healthy. But how in the world are we to find joy in the middle of pain, crisis, and disappointment?

True joy referred to by Scripture is gladness based not on our emotions or circumstances but on our Source—our Source being the firm foundation of Christ. True joy is centered around who Jesus is and His promises to us. Think about it: if our joy is found in Jesus, then our supply remains steady and our reasons for gladness are abundant.

That means that the joyful heart Scripture refers to carries us beyond a moment of laughter and gives us stability in times of pain.

Choosing joy probably won't change our circumstances. But it can change our outlook, which will buffer us from some of our problems' harmful effects.

But if joy is such a powerful tool to our well-being, then the absence of it must work against us. I've seen people harbor bitterness, and eventually the emotional toxicity works itself into their physical bodies, causing all sorts of chronic health issues. We humans are tri-une beings; each of us has a body, a soul (mind, will, and emotions), and a spirit. All three parts make up who we are as individuals, and all three parts are connected, each affecting the others. So you cannot have toxicity lingering in your soul and expect your body not to feel the effect.

In today's society anxiety and depression are rapidly on the rise. (I identify all too well, having had my own bout with anxiety several years ago.) As a whole, it seems as if our society is well on the way to emotional unhealth. We are hurried, shame-laden, social-media obsessed, driven to succeed at all costs, fearful, overextended, over-committed, overworked, and underjoyed. Our nerves and senses are so overstimulated—is it any wonder we are numbing ourselves with everything from alcohol and drugs to food and online shopping in search of relief? I admit I've had to tell myself a few times, *Don't do it! Step away from the Amazon ledge and empty your cart!* In our frantic efforts to make life better, or at least tolerable, we have inadvertently made it worse.

Thirty minutes of watching the news can put us in a bad mood.

It seems that everyone hates everyone, one political party is trying to overthrow the other, wars are waging, hunger is on the rise both at home and abroad, and the world is falling apart—or at least that's what it feels like.

When I was in middle school, my computer teacher told our class that one day computers would run everything so that people would be able to work less. She was only partially right. These days computers do run nearly everything, but we aren't really working less. With smartphones and tablets attached to us like extra appendages, our work never stops, and our peace of mind pays the price.

The other day I turned my television to a news channel and noticed the serious scowl on the reporter's face. I turned up the volume, expecting late-breaking news of a tragedy or threat. But he was only talking about the weather.

We have got to lighten up, laugh more, and smile more. Life is too tough to take it so seriously. Our tension is going to put us in early graves.

In one study, researchers found that when participants were asked to smile (regardless of their real mood), they found more humor in their surroundings than those who were asked to frown.[4] If taking control of our facial muscles by turning a frown into a smile affects our well-being, how much more will taking control of our minds by focusing on God's faithfulness help us stay healthy as we weather life's storms?

OUR FEELINGS OVERFLOW FROM OUR FOCUS.

Lasting joy won't be found in a new car, an improved situation, a bigger home, a better job, or a slimmer body. These things can enhance the happiness that is already there. But they can't affect the foundation of our joy—because joy flows from the fixation of the mind's eye. Joy is a focus long before it's a feeling, and our feelings overflow from our focus.

Jesus Himself modeled this truth for us, as the writer of Hebrews (traditionally believed to be Paul) explained:

> We look away from the natural realm and we fasten our gaze onto Jesus who birthed faith within us and who leads us forward into faith's perfection. His example is this: Because his heart was focused on the joy of knowing that you would be his, he endured the agony of the cross and conquered its humiliation, and now sits exalted at the right hand of the throne of God!
>
> (Heb. 12:2 TPT)

Jesus endured unbelievable suffering by finding strength in His focus. He wasn't fixated on the pain of the cross or the fact that He was dying. He was focused on what the outcome would be, and that focus brought Him joy.

I find that remarkable because my pain is usually all-consuming. When I'm hurting, I have a difficult time concentrating on anything else. But Jesus' ability to focus on joy in the midst of pain tells me it's something that must be learned. Jesus was 100 percent human and 100 percent God. His divinity didn't override His humanity, so He felt the agony of torn muscles, strained breath, a crown of thorns pressed into His skull, not to mention the experience of betrayal, concern for His family and friends, and the sin of all humankind. He endured every ounce of that grueling pain solely because His eyes, blinded by blood, remained fixed on the purpose of the cross. He found joy in the guaranteed outcome that what awaited on the other side of His pain was His victory over sin and death and the purchase of His valuable children. Wow. Just wow.

Focusing on the outcome shapes our perspective differently than focusing on the pain. When we look at the cross, we may see death, but

Jesus saw the life that would come through it. Because of this focus, Jesus knew joy in His pain. We can do that too.

And no, we're not Jesus. We don't have the benefit of divine insight. And we may not know exactly where to focus because we don't fully know the outcome of a particular trial or disappointment. But here's the secret: Jesus does. If we trust that He has a purpose tied to what we're going through and keep our focus on Him, we will find joy.

WHERE IS YOUR STARE?

I like to play tennis. Although I'm not very good, I did play on a recreational team for a couple of years. And one of the techniques my coach drilled into us is looking in the direction that we want to hit the ball. He taught us that our bodies follow our stares. And I learned that was absolutely true. Every time I hit a wild ball, I'd realize I had forgotten to look in the direction I wanted to aim.

> **WHERE IS MY STARE? WHAT ARE MY PHYSICAL EYES AND THE EYES OF MY HEART GAZING UPON? OUR JOY FOLLOWS OUR STARE.**

If you want to find joy in your life, it's worth asking: Where is my stare? What are my physical eyes and the eyes of my heart gazing upon? Our joy follows our stare. Is it on what life used to be, what others have, or the pain you're now feeling?

Haven's health crisis made it especially challenging for me not to fix my eyes on the life I'd once had. I would dream about a few months before when I wasn't worrying if my child would live past her second birthday. I'd long to sip coffee with my girlfriends while our kids played together, and I wondered what I was missing out on back home.

With the unique opportunities provided by social-media apps to peek into other people's lives, we tend to live in comparison mode. Friends' and even strangers' lives often look more glamorous, enjoyable, and exciting than ours. We're tempted to think if only we had their life, it would be easy to be happy. But you can't have roaming eyes and sustain joy—first, because what people show on their news feeds is not nearly as perfect as it may seem, and second, because comparison tends to rob our lives of the joy hidden in them. Here's a truth that I'm learning: No one's life has ever been perfect and easy. Everyone has private internal struggles. We can't pick and choose only the good parts from people's lives and leave the bad. I would love to have a certain American actress turned British princess's long, thick hair, fabulous closet of clothes, and professional chef cooking healthy and organic meals at my disposal. But then I'd also have to accept the criticism she endures, her lack of privacy, and the way she's treated unfairly by the media as well.

Fixing our eyes on only the good in others' lives creates a false reality that steals joy and fosters discontentment. Our lives would be far more enjoyable if we focused on living them instead of on what's happening in someone else's life.

That's exactly what I found in those months in Memphis. When my gaze veered off course, my happi-

YOU CAN'T HAVE ROAMING EYES AND SUSTAIN JOY.

ness level dropped. Mooning over what life had been like back home or what the future might bring stole my joy. I had to learn to find joy in the present. And there truly was joy to be had there—in the hospital stays, the doctor's appointments, and even the hospital food.

We learned to make the best of the situation by laughing and entertaining ourselves. We'd fill our time by seeing who could concoct the grossest combination of Jelly Belly flavors and then, of course, trying to convince the other person to taste it. Casey made up chants about things like Cracker Barrel's beef stew to make Haven laugh. It usually worked, not necessarily because the chants were funny but because he looked so strange doing them.

Once, on our way out of the hospital, Casey accidentally drove through the arm at the parking-garage exit and cracked it in half. Of course, being the honorable people that we are, we kept going. We were too embarrassed to let anyone know what we had done. The next day when we arrived at the hospital, the arm was duct-taped together. We never let Casey live that down.

I can't tell you how much those times of laughter helped us. There was far too much stress in our lives for us to take everything seriously. I imagine there are times when this is true for you too. But we were only able to choose joy because of an inner knowing that God was in control, an internal focus that was lifted high above the pain.

But let me be truthful. That focus didn't always come easily for me. I had to choose to have it and fight to keep it. Some days were so stressful, laughter was the only way we could keep from collapsing under the strain. I remember one day in particular when the tension was so high that I thought I was going to explode. We sat in the hospital cafeteria, waiting as Haven underwent more tests and procedures. Holland was only a couple of weeks old at the time, and trying to tend to a newborn in the hospital all day while calming my one-year-old during procedures was a difficult juggling act. I was intensely grateful to have the help of our mothers, but of course my kids only wanted me, so I constantly felt distracted and pulled in both directions. There just wasn't enough of me to go around.

On this particular day, after walking the halls, pumping breast milk in the bathroom stalls, and eating from the vending machines out of boredom, I found myself in the cafeteria, taking part in one of my favorite pastimes: people watching. It's amazing how much you can guess about people's lives just by pausing long enough to observe. Sitting on a long bench, Casey and I tried to guess where people were from or which celebrities they looked like or what their stories were. It was silly and pointless, but it kept my mind occupied.

In her stroller, Holland started to stir from sleep, then let out a big wail. Checking the clock, I realized it was time for her to eat. I reached in my diaper bag and pulled out a bottle, but I couldn't find any of the nipples that attached to the lid.

You need to know at this point that I don't particularly like the word *nipple*. I find it a bit cringeworthy, and I'm not exactly sure why, except there aren't many situations when the word *nipple* is appropriate. But sometimes it must be used.

"Has anyone seen the nipples to the bottles?" I asked.

"I haven't seen any nipples," my mom responded. "Casey, have you seen the nipples?"

"I haven't seen the nipples. Are they in the diaper bag?" he asked.

My mom's voice grew louder. "Maybe the nipples are in my purse." She dug in her bag and came up empty. "Are the nipples in your purse?" she asked. "Or the nipples could be in the bottom of the stroller. Check the stroller for the nipples."

Holland's hungry wail was getting louder, and I wanted to yell, "For the love of God, people, can you please stop saying the word *nipple?*" Then suddenly, as if we had timed it, a woman with the biggest set of breasts I have ever laid eyes on walked in front of us. I'm not kidding; they were worthy of reverence.

We all quieted. No one moved. My mouth may have dropped open. The baby even paused her screaming, as if she, too, was admiring God's handiwork. Then the thought came to me and I couldn't help but say it out loud: "There they are."

The three of us erupted in laughter, and to this day I am still amazed at the timing of it all. Needless to say, that moment of laughter released my internal pressure valve. I have even wondered if that moment of hilarity was a form of worship.

Don't put away this book because I just related worshiping God to laughing at boobs. Honestly, I'm not being sacrilegious. I'm simply pointing out that choosing joy in the midst of trial honors God. The ability to laugh in the face of pain is a tribute to Him because your heart trusts Him enough to let go of worry and let joy in.

I guess you could say that's His joy becoming your strength. It's saying, "God, I trust You enough to lighten up. I relax my clenched fists and choose to live openhanded, with palms up, receiving Your joy."

Choosing joy may not change your circumstance, but it will change your heart and enable you to endure.

OUR JOY FOCUS

Joy is not discovered; it's developed. When we choose joy and then make the same choice over and over again, we are developing our joy focus. A habitual response of joy is what sets our feet on the way to victory, which is why it should be a regular fixture not only in our homes, schools, and workplaces, but also in our worship.

JOY IS NOT DISCOVERED; IT'S DEVELOPED.

My husband, Casey, has a great sense of humor. He can make going to the dentist enjoyable. And one of my favorite things to do is watch a comedy with him; his laugh is so contagious I find it funnier than the movie.

Casey uses his sense of humor in his sermons to disarm people and keep them engaged. Most people respond well to this approach.

However, a man who attended our church in its early days once pulled him aside and said sternly, "You need to get more serious."

I think that man's response said more about him than it did about Casey's approach to sermons. While salvation through the gospel is indeed a serious matter, so is joy! After all, God created us with the capacity for healthy humor, and Jesus brought the good news that brought "great joy for all the people" (Luke 2:10)! We need more of that kind of joy, not less, in our churches as well as in our homes and our cities.

I think people tend to see God with pursed lips and a pinched brow, but joy is a major part of God's character. God Himself tells us in His Word to make joy and revelry a part of our worship:

> Lift up a great shout of joy to the Lord!
> Go ahead and do it—everyone, everywhere!
> As you serve him, be glad and worship him.
> Sing your way into his presence with joy!
> And realize what this really means—
> we have the privilege of worshiping the Lord our God.
> (Ps. 100:1–3 TPT)

How sad it would be if in a misguided attempt to be reverent, we lose the strength God wants to give us through joyful, lighthearted worship.

429,120 MINUTES

Choosing joy can be a life-giving, lifesaving possibility. James 1:2 tells us to count life's pain as joy. Joyful pain—talk about an oxymoron.

But in my experience, at least, the joy was right there with the pain. It was one of the things that made the suffering bearable.

Our journey with Haven's illness lasted from December 25, 1998, until October 19, 1999. Not one of those minutes was easy. That's 429,120 minutes of bad news, sleepless nights, an ambulance ride, hospital stays, vomit, chemotherapy, tears, hospital food, stress, and more suffering than I ever want to see again in my lifetime. So many days of hell. I got through them not by waiting on the feeling of joy but by choosing it.

One afternoon at our hotel, Haven needed the bandage changed on her Hickman line (the tube attached to her chest, where medicines were administered). Casey had always done this, but he was away, so it was now my turn. My mother-in-law and I read the written instructions on how to remove the old bandage, clean the incision, and apply another sterile pad. We tried our best to follow the directions perfectly, but Haven wouldn't cooperate. She kicked and screamed and flailed her body in every direction as I tried to remove the bandage.

Anxiety was building in my gut. This was far more painful for me than it was for her. When the bandage was finally off, I tried to clean the area and put on the new sterile bandage, but she refused to be touched. My mother-in-law tried her best to hold her down, but it was like wrestling a bear. My hands shook and tears flowed down my face as I fought to apply that little piece of gauze.

After wrestling with Haven for at least twenty minutes, I finally got the bandage in place. Releasing a giant sigh of relief, I lay back on the hotel floor with my hands over my face. Silence reigned for just a moment, punctuated only by a few sniffles from Haven. Then my mother-in-law cracked, "Do you need a smoke?"

"Dear God, yes!" I replied with a chuckle. Even though neither of us smoked. That triggered the laughter I needed so desperately. I laughed until tears of joy, not sadness, trickled down the side of my face onto the carpet beneath me.

Crying can be a good thing. It can cleanse your body and mind of stress. But though there is a time for weeping, there is also a time for joy. At that moment, I needed joy far more than I needed hysterical tears.

I knew the road ahead would be long and that there would be many occasions for serious tears. For this moment, I accepted my mother-in-law's attempt to make light of our stress by cracking a joke. It worked. It minimized the problem I could do nothing about, and my mood turned from sadness to joy in an instant.

Feelings are important, but they can also betray us and lead us astray. Don't wait to choose joy until you feel joyful. God gave us a powerful will to choose the right thing even when our feelings don't agree. The ability to discern the irony of humor in a given situation is a gift from God to lighten our load, and I believe we should take full advantage of it. I'm not talking about ill-timed jokes and misplaced humor, and I'm not trying to be dismissive of anyone's pain. But I know that getting through life's challenges means not giving them more power than they deserve. Tension and worry are never going to help us.

WHY WORRY?

Worry gives us a false sense of control over our problems. It's the nanny babysitting our issues. But our peace is its high-priced hourly rate. By worrying about a problem, we keep it alive in our minds, afraid that if we stop thinking about it, it will never change. Who will be focused on our problem if we're not? But the truth is, worry doesn't change a thing, and the sense of empowerment it brings is completely fake.

I wonder if sometimes we focus on our problems by worrying because we're afraid to focus on joy. It sounds twisted, doesn't it? But I catch myself doing this more than I care to admit. When something is weighing on me, my mind may momentarily focus on other things and I'll forget the problem. But when I realize this has happened, I'll quickly grow uncomfortable with the absence of worry, and out of fear, I'll recall the issue that's causing me stress.

INSTEAD OF STRESSING, I NEED TO FOCUS ON GOD'S SOVEREIGNTY OVER MY SITUATION.

I don't like the feeling of worry, but I don't like having a problem and not doing something about it, even if the only thing I can do about it is worry.

What's the alternative? Instead of stressing, I need to focus on God's sovereignty over my situation. I'm not sitting idle when I do this. I'm taking action by choosing my focus and receiving joy. As we learn to trust God, we will see that joy is the gift and worry is the thief.

Moving Forward in Joy

Maybe there's a situation that caused you pain a decade ago, and you didn't choose joy in the midst of it. You got bitter and you find that this choice still affects you today. But time can often give us better vision to see how we should have responded in the past. So you still have time to change your focus and choose joy. If you're still breathing, you have an opportunity to change your outlook on any past or present problem or disappointment. Focusing on the pain will marry you to it, leaving you stuck in Harran, when the promised land awaits. Choosing joy will benefit your heart and move you forward.

Psalm 30:5 says that "weeping may last through the night, but joy comes with the morning" (NLT).

The promise of something new, a new hope, a new day, a new joy behind every long night of the soul, is given to us through Christ's redemption.

For some of us, the sun has risen and joy has come, but we keep pushing it away and pulling the covers back over our heads. There is an appropriate time for sadness and mourning, but don't dwell there longer than you should. Don't stick around Harran, complaining about what used to be, how good you had it, or what did or didn't happen for you.

Harran is not your inheritance. And every day that you choose Harran, you sink yourself deeper into the parched desert sand. But one choice to change your outlook excavates your feet and moves you forward with a lighter, freer, happier heart.

No matter what your circumstances, joy is always an option.

SIX

AN UNLIKELY WEAPON

The day began like any other, only this day marked ten weeks of chemotherapy treatments for Haven. The doctors had a full series of tests planned to evaluate how her body was responding to her specific treatment. Basically, the tests would reveal if the chemotherapy was doing its job. They told us not to worry. Not possible. They told us that these tests were given to all their brain-tumor patients. Still not possible. They suspected the results would come back favorable and that nothing would need to change in Haven's chemotherapy protocol. Their speech sounded rehearsed, like something they told all their patients, and it didn't feel believable. I had no reason to suspect a problem, but the very act of taking a test meant a failing grade was possible. That made me nervous. These tests would determine my child's future.

Shortly after arriving at the hospital, we put Haven in the doctor's care and then started our waiting marathon. After just thirty minutes I was ready to fake a leg cramp and quit. My imagination begged to run wild like an out-of-control child as I did my best to keep it disciplined. Again, not possible.

One hour down, and still we waited. Two hours, still waiting. Three hours, four hours, five hours. Was it normal for these tests to take so long?

To occupy my time and distract myself, I walked the halls of the hospital, visited the gift shop twice, fed Holland, and struggled to focus on conversation with Casey and my mother-in-law. We all talked, but no one was really listening.

The clock crept at a snail's pace, and the waiting was starting to kill me. Bombarded by fear, I needed some space to breathe. I spotted a vacant window nearby, walked over to it, and started to quietly sing a worship song. It was all I knew to do. I needed to tap into the well of the Holy Spirit so His living water could quench my thirst for peace. I needed to be reminded that He is good and powerful and sovereign—even over cancer.

A Spiritual Fight

In this world, there is an active, ongoing war being waged for our worship and our praise. This battle is not one of flesh and blood, but a spiritual fight against the powers of darkness. Its objectives are our attention and reverence, and it is active every day, every minute of every hour. The crowned winner achieves the prize of our focus and thus calls the shots in our life.

We are all in this battle whether we realize it or not. Whether we choose it or not. Whether we knowingly engage in it or not. To be victors, we need to know exactly what biblical praise and worship are and why they are so important.

So, let's take just a moment to define them. First, they are two different acts but can accompany each other. The biblical words for worship mean "to kiss the hand,"[1] "to bow down in reverence."[2]

The words for praise mean "to give thanks, boast, commend, honor, and sing praise."[3]

You can see by their definitions that praise and worship are more than just singing songs in church. If worship means to kiss the hand of God in reverence, how often does my time with Him reflect that? And is what I'm giving Him truly worship? Ouch.

Those definitions take it beyond just something we do on Sunday to an ongoing lifestyle of gratitude, honoring and boasting of God no matter where we are. Both praise and worship begin in our hearts as an overflow of what God means to us.

Standing at that window while waiting on those test results, worship was my lifeline. I didn't need a dark room, a prerecorded song, or a church band to lead me. All I needed was for my heart to desire to lift Jesus above my anxiety. It really is that simple. So I took time to kiss the hand of God, revere Him more than I did the tests, and adore Him for all He'd brought me through. By bowing my soul low before Him, I was saying, "I can't, but You can!" Doing so strengthened my trust that He would faithfully bring me through this too.

Being a pastor means I am in the church a lot. When I have opportunities to participate in corporate worship, I admit that sometimes I end up going through the motions instead of truly engaging. I'll catch myself thinking about what I'm going to eat for lunch after church, how the coffee I'm sipping tastes, or how badly my fingernail polish is chipping. I suspect I'm not the only one who does this.

I wonder if we would put more weight on worship if we realized the magnitude of its power. I fear that all too often we've become apathetic and disengaged. I'm certainly not judging or condemning anyone, but every day I see people whose lives are hanging on by a thread, and yet they're forfeiting connection to their powerful lifeline because they don't understand its importance. They'll cruise into church and spend more energy putting the right amount of sugar in their coffee than they do prioritizing worship. *What's the big deal?* they wonder. *At least I made it to church.* Yes, but have they missed an opportunity to commune with God, to become spiritually aligned, and to hear His voice? I say this because I care. I'm tired of watching people all too often get pulverized in the spiritual fight because they don't understand the importance of connecting with God through honor and adoration.

Life is hard enough. We have bills and bad days and are in a constant war with our spiritual enemy. Why disregard time with our Source? Out of sight and out of mind doesn't apply to the battle we face. We can disengage, but that doesn't mean the battle ends. No, it's still going on. We're just losing.

Worship and praise are weapons of war against our adversary because by lifting God higher, we push the enemy lower. But it also strengthens the tender, open-heart bond between heavenly Father and earthly child and is therefore one of the most sacred things we can do.

Is it no wonder that darkness contends for our worship? Worship is the breath of life to our souls.

Every morning when I wake up, I try to spend time reflecting on God's goodness, ability, and worthiness. For me it is a passage into His presence, and I need connection with my Savior every day.

Struggle, disappointment, and pain tend to dehydrate my soul. It is through worship that the Holy Spirit's well of living water immerses our souls and satisfies our inner thirst with His Being. My challenges also tend to eclipse God's power in my mind. Praise turns my spiritual eyes back to God's ability and stokes the joy that might be fading in my heart. Speaking or singing words of gratitude and appreciation for what God has done turns our mourning into joy. Without engaged praise, therefore, we become parched bones, roaming, searching, seeking, but unsatisfied and disappointed by what we thought would give us peace and strength.

I wonder how many disengaged believers would say that they expected more from Christianity. Is it possible that their unmet expectations are a result of self-help instead of true worship and surrender?

Worship changes the landscape of our hearts because it tunes us in to the frequency of the Holy Spirit's voice. I can pinpoint specific times in my life when I heard Him speak to me while I was engaged with Him through worship. Those times altered what I believed about myself, gave me the direction I was asking for, or settled the anxiety in my soul. More than once in worship, I've heard God call me "daughter," giving me a sense of identity, something I've struggled with, and saying that I am enough for Him. I can honestly say that my identity as a cherished daughter of God was shaped in my times with Him as I sang, wept, and focused

WORSHIP CHANGES THE LANDSCAPE OF OUR HEARTS BECAUSE IT TUNES US IN TO THE FREQUENCY OF THE HOLY SPIRIT'S VOICE.

on the good Father He is. When we feel afraid, beat up by life or questioning our value and ability, if we carve out time to be in the presence of Jesus, it will right our minds and keep us on course.

TRUE WORSHIP

If we want to be true worshipers, then we must oust everything other than God from the throne of our hearts. No one else deserves that seat. I admit that sometimes I grant rule to my own will, my emotions, or unmet expectations.

Lifting God higher than our pain puts things in their rightful place. God is bigger than cancer, bigger than test results, bigger than divorce, bigger than debt, bigger than you or me. We lift God high when we raise our praise. This doesn't mean that we don't allow ourselves to feel the pain or deal with our emotions. It's unhealthy to suppress what God wants to heal. It simply means that we put Christ above and at the center and make all other things peripheral. When we do that, we are worshiping and praising Him.

A lifestyle of worship is one that strives to honor God in our decisions, actions, and words. And note that word *strives*. We don't have to wait until we reach perfection to worship. That is a lie of the enemy to keep us from attaching to God. Human perfection is 100 percent impossible anyway. So we simply need to take a deep breath and exhale condemnation. God knows what we did last night. And last month. And ten years ago. He wants us to worship Him anyway.

God lovingly receives our imperfect hearts in their present condition if we come to Him contrite and humble. But He loves us too much to leave us as He finds us, so He calls us to worship, because worship helps make us more like Christ.

Don't wait until you change to worship. Worship so that you *can* change.

NOT FEELING IT?

Remember, worship is essentially an overflow of a submitted heart enthralled by God. It is spillover from someone who realizes that her very breath is on loan from Him and therefore uses it to bless the Sustainer of her soul.

But what about the times when the overflow isn't flowing? When we just don't feel it? That's when we must choose to praise God despite our feelings. Because regardless of circumstance, He is still worthy. And by choosing to lift God high, we'll be given the strength we need.

Many times I elevate my circumstances above God's ability to change them. I'm not sure why I do this. Maybe it's because my circumstances feel more real, more concrete, practically immovable. Whatever the reason, I basically bow down to them, serve them, stand in awe of them, even bless them. I don't mean to or plan to do this, but I definitely do it, and then my situation becomes my all-consuming focus. Before I know it my shoulders are tense, my anxiety has spiked, and my heart rate accelerates because I've allowed fear or my problems to rule my heart.

That's exactly what happened to me while we waited for the test results. They were all I could think about. *What if* kept repeating in my mind.

And that's why I turned to worship. The deep in me called out to the deep in Christ because I needed more than a brisk walk around the hospital could provide. Nothing but worship answers the thirst in us that can only be satiated through an innermost attachment to God. Attempting to fill the void with anything else just makes us thirstier.

Several other substances or activities might have helped ease my angst that day. Xanax might have taken the edge off. A half hour of yoga or a cocktail with an extra shot might have relieved some of the tension. A piece of cake might have made me feel a little better, and some online shopping while I waited might have distracted me. But after an hour or so, I'd be right back where I started, possibly even worse off, because not one of those has the power to truly change me. Worship does.

What Happens When We Worship?

Worship is a holy exchange that trades our dead end for God's possibilities, giving us the courage to break away from our disappointments. Worship also thins the veil that separates the physical and spiritual worlds and positions our hearts to see God more clearly, like dilating our spiritual pupils. It reveals what might have been hidden before by tuning us in to the frequency of heaven. At any given moment there is a heavenly conversation going on about our circumstance. Have you ever considered that God has direction for everything you face, and worship is a way to listen in?

There is no substitute for the way that worship softens, molds, and poises the human heart for God's presence. It keeps our hearts malleable to receive His fertile promise that there is more beyond our pain. Our spiritual senses heighten in worship. The ears of our spirits hear the sound of His whisper: *Don't give up. Keep walking. There is more!*

What do I mean by more? More goodness than we now know. More power than we've yet to experience. More strength, more grace, more love, and more life beyond our present. Where we stand is not the end. No, it is a crossroads to the more that is ahead. It reminds us that greater power than we will ever understand resides in us through the Holy Spirit as He reaches through the veil and extends His heart.

When we worship Jesus, we are reminded that no spiritual weapon wielded against us either now or in our future will have the power to destroy us because we'll be hidden in Christ and attached to the Vine. Once we choose to believe, the stronghold of fear starts to crumble. Piece by piece it falls as we receive His words in faith.

WORSHIPING WHILE WE WAIT

Looking out of that window in St. Jude, I placed all the pent-up fear inside me before the Lord on an altar of worship. I worshiped while I waited. And it prepared me for what God had in store next. When God's timetable is not our own, there is nothing more productive we can do. In worship we will find renewed strength to move beyond discouragement and we will be prepared for what He has in store.

As I sang by the hospital window that morning, God prepared me to offer strength to another woman who was waiting there, holding a young child. She approached me, and the first thing I noticed was the strain marking her face and the look of bitterness in her eyes. "You're Haven's mom, right? We haven't met, but our daughters are on the same chemotherapy protocol." Nudging her chin down toward the child resting in her arms, she said, "This is Emily. She also has a brain tumor."

Little Emily had just come from a session of radiation and hung lethargic in her mother's arms. I asked her mother how Emily was doing, and I will never forget the anguish in her response. "The treatment didn't work. Her tumor came back. Our last hope was radiation, but it doesn't seem to be working either. I don't know what else to do!"

This woman had no idea that Haven's tests today would reveal whether the treatment was working for her or not. She was clueless that what she was saying could have sent me into a downward spiral of fear. Instead, I was pierced with compassion for Emily's mom, who stood in front of me wrecked with hopelessness. It broke my heart that while we were in the same situation, she didn't seem to have the same kind of relationship with a God who wooed her to worship in times of pain. I couldn't imagine life without that intimate connection with God to center my eyes and align my heart with what He says about my circumstance. I, too, would have been wrecked with hopelessness.

As much as I wished I could, I couldn't heal little Emily. I had nothing to offer her mom but prayer. But prayer isn't a paltry offering. We aren't bereft when it is all we have to give. We are amply equipped, in fact, armed with the mighty weapons of our warfare. So, I reached out to this beautiful woman. Putting my hands on her shoulders, I asked God to heal Emily and to reveal Himself to her mom and give her hope for a good future. As I did, tears coursed down her face and mine. When I finished, she thanked me and walked away.

ALL HELL TREMBLES WHEN WE TRULY WORSHIP.

I never saw Emily's mom again, but I have prayed that seeds of hope were planted in her heart in that moment and that they grew into an intimate relationship with God. I hope that relationship was forged by her running to Him with her pain instead of blaming Him for it.

Worshiping God poised my heart for that encounter with Emily's mom. Even while I battled my own fear, God gave me strength and courage to help someone else. He filled me, and it spilled onto those around me. Worship created the exchange.

Worship opens our hearts to receive what He has for us. That's why all hell trembles when we truly worship. Satan knows how effective this weapon is in our warfare against him.

THE STORM UNLEASHED

It was now five in the afternoon. By this time, Haven was with us, but the doctors had asked us to stick around for the final test results. The waiting room was empty except for us, and that made me nervous.

Why would the doctors leave us waiting so long if the results were normal? We left our fears unspoken, but we knew in our hearts that something was wrong.

It was storming outside. Through the walls we heard pelting rain and the clap of thunder. I had an odd feeling, as if doom was brewing beneath the exterior surface of our lives and was about to let loose. My jumbled thoughts contradicted themselves. *Somebody please come get us. . . . No, I don't want to know. I'd rather stay here in denial.*

Finally a nurse peeked around the corner and called us to a room where a team of doctors awaited. Their expressions of pity and regret instantly told me the results weren't good. My breath became labored before they had even spoken a word. Once they started, I wanted to crumble inside. The tumor had come back, they said, but this time it was inoperable. There was nothing left that they could do. They said they were shocked and hadn't seen this coming. Neither had I.

At that point our choices were limited. We could try high-dose chemotherapy, which they didn't recommend, or we could take Haven home and keep her comfortable until the end.

Those were the words I had never wanted to hear. *The end.* It sounded so final. So hopeless. So nonnegotiable. So hard to accept. I squeezed my eyes shut and listened to Casey ask what I didn't want to know. "How long does she have left?" The doctors guessed anywhere from six weeks to six months. As we prepared to walk out their door, they left us with one final thought. "You need to be prepared for a very hard death."

I wanted to respond with bitterness, like Emily's mom. I wanted to yell at the top of my lungs, "This isn't fair! Why didn't you make it work? Don't speak those words over my child's life!" I wanted to lunge over the exam table and force the doctors to take their words back. After all the pain, all the worry, all the ups and downs of the past months, was this how it was going to end? All the believing and praying and choosing joy for *this*?

I refused to believe this was God's plan. It couldn't be. I wouldn't allow it. It was Satan's plan, and I would fight him with everything I had.

Leaving their office, we walked to the hospital elevator in complete silence. When the doors closed, my mother-in-law demanded in a quivering voice, "Don't give up on God! Do you hear me? Don't give up on God!"

I wasn't giving up. I'd never even consider that. But I didn't want to accept what life was demanding of me. And I didn't know how I would get through the coming months.

Outside, the storm had turned into forceful, swirling wind that howled and pushed against our car. We didn't make it far down the road before tornado sirens sounded across the city. Forced to park under an interstate overpass for shelter, we waited in silence as flood-water rose halfway up our tires. The wind was so deafening that I thought it may carry us away, and a small part of me wished it would. Then I would be free of this nightmare.

What a living metaphor this weather was—torrential downpour, rising water, and crashing thunder unleashing around me just as it was inside me. We were still hunkered under that sturdy overpass, but the fighter in me needed to fight. In my mind's eye I was standing out in the rain and wind, pumping my fist and wailing, "I will not allow you to defeat us! You will not overcome us!"

The fight drained out of me as the storm weakened. Instead of railing against it, I hid my soul under the shelter of Christ's wings. He would protect me. He would protect Haven. But then my peace shattered again as I glanced back at Haven resting in her car seat, completely clueless to the fate just spoken over her. But I was resolute. I had to be. *I won't accept death.*

Denial quickly moved to bargaining. I reminded God that I had served Him throughout high school, had been a leader in my youth ministry, had brought myself to church every Wednesday night and Sunday morning, sometimes even on Sunday night. I reasoned that my faithfulness justified answered prayer. I asked to be honored for every hour spent on my knees, every time I'd said no to peer pressure, every church service I'd attended, every phone call of encouragement I'd made to the girls I mentored, every unseen sacrifice, every tithe, every offering—for all of it.

I begged Jesus to grant me this one thing. *Heal my child. Do a miracle for me, the girl who has loved You all her life.* I leveraged my faithfulness to move God's faithfulness. I repeated this argument a thousand times in my mind on the way to the apartment and as we took shelter in our neighbor's home downstairs. The storm had picked up again, and our apartment was on the top floor, surrounded by windows.

The elderly neighbor was kind, but I never got her name. She tried to make small talk, but we weren't in the talking mood. She had no idea of the news we had just been given.

As I waited for the howling winds to stop, I repeated my silent litany: *Do a miracle because of my sacrifice to You.* But even as I did, I knew the truth, that God didn't need me to leverage my faithfulness to move His. He is faithful even when I'm not. He doesn't ask us to prove ourselves before He loves us or moves on our behalf. In reality we can do nothing that merits His faithfulness. But He loves us. He loved us long before we ever loved Him. And His faithfulness exceeds any shred we could ever muster.

Even though I knew all this, desperation still compelled me to get God's attention. So I kept praying, *God, remember my sacrifices.*

Of course, I knew He was already listening, watching, aching, and involved in this with me, but somehow it gave me a sense of power on a day when I felt helpless.

When the storm finally let up and we made it to our apartment, I immediately grabbed my Bible and opened it. My soul was like the deer David described in Psalm 42, desperately panting for water. I longed for the washing of God's Word over me.

I opened the worn leather book at random, and my eyes fell on Psalm 20:

> May he remember every gift you have given him
> and celebrate every sacrifice of love you have shown him. . . .
> May God give you every desire of your heart
> and carry out your every plan as you go to battle. . . .
> Yes, God will answer your prayers and we will praise him! . . .
> By his mighty hand miracles will manifest
> through his saving strength.
>
> (vv. 3–6 TPT)

God answered my desperation with those words from His Word. I stood from the couch with the Bible in my hand and read the verses out loud to Casey and his mom. With each sentence my voice got stronger and my resolve deeper. God had heard my cry and would answer me. He'd told me through Psalm 20 that He would remember. But I knew He had never forgotten.

In the days to come, I held tight to this fresh word as if it were my lifeline. When dread overwhelmed me, I spoke this psalm and praised God, recalling His power and ability. When anxiety attacked me—and it did with a vengeance—I took shelter under His wings by worshiping.

When the floodwater rises, run to His protective cover through worship. Wait out the storm in His presence. When the sirens sound, get low. Hit your knees, and look to Him for deliverance.

All that night and the next morning, cancer whispered in my ear, *I'm undefeatable.* It was hard not to let it rule my thoughts and emotions. It demanded my worship.

Satan uses fear, disappointment, and unchanging circumstances as weapons against you. The best way to fight the battle *for* your worship is *to* worship. It is your weapon in the fight.

> The weapons we fight with are not the weapons of the world. On the contrary, they have divine power to demolish strongholds. We demolish arguments and every pretension that sets itself up against the knowledge of God, and we take captive every thought to make it obedient to Christ.
>
> (2 Cor. 10:4–5)

A stronghold can be defined simply as anything that has a strong hold over you, be it fear, disappointment, or addiction. Strongholds are formed by believing a lie from the enemy. He may tell us we have no hope left. By continually believing that lie, we've set ourselves up to become shackled in a stronghold of hopelessness. The way strongholds are broken is by receiving and believing God's truth. And worship is a powerful vehicle to hear that truth.

WAIT OUT THE STORM IN HIS PRESENCE. WHEN THE SIRENS SOUND, GET LOW. HIT YOUR KNEES, AND LOOK TO HIM FOR DELIVERANCE.

Here is the sobering part: we are the only ones who have the power to partner with Jesus to set us free. No one else can do it for us. We must choose. But here's the encouraging part: because we can partner with Jesus, freedom is within our reach.

Satan will try anything to bind us with fear. We must close the doors of our minds to the enemy and not allow him to use them as his playground. The best way I know how to do this is to worship. As we lift God high, monsters of debt, disease, divorce, and disappointment shrink in comparison to His glorious might. As we look to Him, suddenly we see things as they really are.

WHEN LIFE IS AT STAKE

The morning after the storm, we returned to the hospital for our final instructions. We informed the doctors that we had decided to take Haven home to Louisiana. They agreed it was the best choice. We thanked them for all they had done in their efforts to heal our child, but we were taking her to the Great Physician.

Pulling away from our Memphis apartment for the final time was like walking on a tightrope with no safety net. I had come to see the hospital and doctors as my security. I looked back one last time and said, "God, You're all I have."

When God is your only hope, it's like being carried across a tightrope in His arms. It's far easier to believe that He won't drop you when your life isn't at stake. There's room for failure when there's a safety net.

You'd choose any other way if you had a choice. You'd even take the long way around. But sometimes life leaves you no option. It's God or nothing.

I've come to see this as one of life's most priceless gifts. And I really mean that. When I have options, too often I find myself walking casually with God, sometimes trailing behind, sometimes walking ahead, and sometimes, like Terah and Abraham, stopping altogether.

But when God is my only way across, I hang on for dear life. I'm focused on His every move. He can't flinch without me feeling it.

SOMETIMES LIFE LEAVES YOU NO OPTION. IT'S GOD OR NOTHING.

Desperation forces us to cling hard, pray strong, fight fierce. And here's the payoff: this intense focus reveals dimensions of His character that a casual glance won't catch. Nearness like this melds our hearts to His like two sheets of steel welded together. Desperation is painful, but true worship is forged in the midst of it, the kind of worship that tears down the strongholds and sets captives free. Chains break in our praise.

A Reprieve and a Setback

We moved home ready to engage in the battle of fear and disbelief and to leave room for God to work a miracle. Our home became a sanctuary of worship. Now that she was off chemotherapy, Haven was eating and sleeping well and feeling better than ever. For a brief moment in time, she seemed like a normal child. She even took a few steps behind a push toy.

Several weeks after we moved home, Haven's pediatric oncologist from St. Jude called to check on her. I told him of her progress, and he had no words to explain why she wasn't declining quickly, which is what they had expected. Then he said the words I will never forget. "It looks like you have gotten your miracle."

Gotten my miracle? Could it be true? I hung up the phone and cried. I couldn't believe this statement had come out of her doctor's mouth. Had God really healed our child? Was the battle finally over? It looked that way for a week or more—until the day that everything turned.

It happened on a humid Louisiana afternoon in July. Our church staff had planned a picnic at a local park. There would be barbecue, music, friends with their chairs circled together, catching up on one another's lives—a few sacred hours where work was put to the side. After being removed from our friends for six months, I could hardly wait to see everyone again.

All was calm that morning as we dressed and loaded into our Nissan Pathfinder. En route to the park, I glanced to the back seat to see Haven shaking in her car seat. In the time it took for me to climb to the back seat, her shaking became uncontrollable and her legs and hands started turning blue. Quickly I unfastened her seat belt and pulled her into my lap. As she shook and cried, I prayed.

Casey turned our car immediately in the direction of the hospital. He drove urgently through Baton Rouge's bumper-to-bumper traffic, rolling over medians, running red lights, and laying on his horn to signal people to move out of our way. With every passing minute Haven's body turned a darker shade of blue and I prayed harder. Casey grabbed our cell phone and called 911. The dispatcher orchestrated an ambulance to meet us in a parking lot a few miles away.

Speeding to the hospital in that ambulance, the sirens blaring around us, my thoughts wrestled with faith and disbelief. Spurred by her doctor's pronouncement, I'd wanted to believe God had done a miracle. Now I didn't know what to think.

I understand if you might think I'd been naive or in denial or even delusional to believe she was healed. But I wasn't—not really. I'd been fully aware that Haven would die without a miracle from Jesus. So every day, all day, we had prayed, worshiped, and believed God's promises of healing.

What would you do? Would you move home and prepare your heart to watch your child painfully deteriorate? Would you start planning a funeral for some time in the next six weeks to six months?

I wasn't in denial. I knew the truth behind what I saw and heard. But I also knew that I served a God who could conquer cancer. In Him I had put my trust, my hope, my belief, my thoughts, and my energy. Isn't that what faith is—fixing our spiritual eyes on the unseen as a fact that we will soon see? This is exactly what I had done. Speeding to the hospital in an ambulance was hard for me to reconcile.

We ended up staying a week in Our Lady of the Lake Hospital because Haven had contracted an infection that led to sepsis in her blood. We were back to square one.

And on this fertile ground, disappointment can grow wild. When there was hope and then suddenly there's not. When you take one step forward but two, three, four steps back. When all the progress you feel you've accomplished is lost in one act, one decision, one moment.

But this is not the time to become entangled in the weeds of disappointment. This is the time to rise up in faith despite what you see. This is the time to set your face forward and plant your feet like never before on the solid promises of God. These are some of life's defining moments when you choose at your crossroads of discouragement and hope which path you will walk. This was one of those moments for me.

One morning during our stay, Dr. Smith, the local pediatric oncologist who became Haven's interim doctor, visited our room with a team of interns. I had heard about her brusque, tell-it-like-it-is personality but hadn't had much of an encounter with her yet. As the team of doctors peered into our room from the hallway, she explained the facts of our situation to the group. "Haven is a terminal patient. She only has several more weeks of life."

Dr. Smith's blunt pronouncement floored me. She spoke it so plainly, as if I weren't standing right next to her. She gave the interns a few more details of our case, then moved to the next room without saying a word. Just like that she had set off a bomb and left me to deal with the carnage of grief.

I had to fight to recover from that moment, but I refused to allow her callousness to hurt me. I turned on worship music, raised my hands to heaven, and decided none of this would deter my faith. I knew the facts as well as anyone, but face forward, I determined I would continue to live in trust, connected to my Savior, feeding my soul His sustenance. I refused to wallow in her words. I would not let them persuade me to lose faith. Whether Haven lived or died was in His hands, but I would worship my way through the process.

EQUIPPED FOR BATTLE

The dynamic of worship is clear and dependable. Those who stay in an attitude of worship are eventually transformed from the inside out. Broken hearts offered to God are put back together. Unbelieving minds are encouraged. Angry spirits are softened. Blurry vision is aligned with God's perspective. God's living water courses through shrunken, dehydrated veins.

True worship and praise bring life. Not simply breathing, but moving forward. Not stuck in Harran, sinking in pain like quicksand. True worship brings victory as well. When we worship, we are fighting for our lives and souls, not hunkered in a foxhole just trying to survive or looking for a white flag to wave.

May worship always be our response to bad news. When it is, the praise we offer as a sacrifice to God will change the spiritual atmosphere to victory. Together, right now, let's decide that staying mentally defeated is never an option. I have learned from experience that it takes more mental and emotional energy to stay in a place of defeat than it does to trust Jesus. A defeated mind is exhausted and depleted. Like a hamster on a wheel, it runs hard but gets nowhere.

I HAVE LEARNED FROM EXPERIENCE THAT IT TAKES MORE MENTAL AND EMOTIONAL ENERGY TO STAY IN A PLACE OF DEFEAT THAN IT DOES TO TRUST JESUS.

God did not design us to live that way. Through Jesus we have a spiritual inheritance that seats us next to Christ in heaven, at God's right hand of authority. We are destined to reign with Christ over our enemy (Eph. 2:6). When so much has been handed to us, why would we settle for living beneath our rank? It is in our power through Christ to rise up and set our minds on things above, where we have already overcome even when our victory has not yet come to fruition. Did you catch that important part of the strategy? We rise even before we see change.

Proverbs 31 talks about the woman of noble character. While I used to see her as intimidating and slightly annoying, I've realized she is really just like us, an ordinary woman who serves an extraordinary God. But this ordinary woman is a fighter. Maybe that's why I've come to like her. She doesn't wait for life to happen to her; she goes out to meet it. For example, she rises while it is still night (v. 15). She gets up from her slumber and sets food on her table for her household and others.

Now, I need my eight hours. I'm not one to get up in the wee hours of the morning unless a child is sick or I'm catching an early flight, and even then, I dread those early hours. But what if this woman is showing us more than just getting out of bed and cooking breakfast for our families while it is still dark? What if the "night" Proverbs refers to is the dark night of the soul? What if the meal she offers her family is the sustenance from her time rising to meet Christ? What if it was prepared with the grit and determination that she's developed by not bowing to fear in darkness?

She is teaching us to rise in worship during dark times. When light is barely visible and our strength and hope fail, let us turn to God to give us everything we need and more. The defeated ones desperately need someone to give them hope. Where else will it come from but from those of us who have a direct lifeline to eternal hope?

This is the person God has created you and me to be. Not a shrinking violet with slumping shoulders, heavy under the weight of defeat. And certainly not the one who bows out of the battle, forfeiting her chance at victory. Too often I find myself starting with valiant effort and then stopping because I don't see anything changing. That kind of apathy doesn't stop the war. It just robs us of the victory.

A. W. Tozer wrote, "The idea that this world is a playground instead of a battleground has now been accepted in practice by the vast majority of . . . Christians."[4]

I understand that life can be tough on us. There have been times I was ridden with so much anxiety I wondered how I would get through the day. But in the middle of whatever storms you are facing, remember that you have fight in you. You are a worshiper, a mighty woman equipped with a sound mind who raises her banner high, declaring that she is on the winning side.

We praise the God who fights our battles, and we take shelter under His standard of victory. We rise up in strength, knowing that though the tide may not turn overnight, we are assured of victory in the end. God is always our Champion and has equipped us for battle. If you don't hear anything else, hear this: If we pull back the sling and launch the smooth stone of His Word directly at the enemy's forehead, it will make contact. He will fall. And we will drag his dead body off our path and keep walking.

This kind of grit is not only granted to the best among us, but to any of us who chooses to rise up in worship amid the storms of our lives. May we be careful not to fight the wrong battle by turning our hearts against God. Instead, wage war against the one who has the stain of fault still lingering on his fingers. Turn your anger and disappointment against Satan and your worship and praise toward God.

To this day I am a passionate worshiper. I can't keep my body still. My hands immediately shoot high in the air, and my voice rings out loudly, even if a bit off-key. I don't care.

It's not a performance. It's an act of overflowing gratitude. I have been through a valley of pain and been brought out of it inch by inch by inch. Yes, I have scars, but I am still worshiping because I know where I would be today without God's sustaining presence. I am forever indebted, and I can't help but express my appreciation and praise for His love.

Like David, I continually ask the Lord in wonder, "Who am I, Sovereign LORD, and what is my family, that you have brought me this far?" (2 Sam. 7:18–19).

SEVEN

THEOLOGY LESSONS

"I was waiting on this phone call. I knew it would come soon," said Dr. Smith one mid-July morning. I had reached out to her because Haven was showing increasing signs of discomfort that Tylenol no longer eased.

"It's a downward spiral that only gets worse from here," she continued. "I'm warning you that it's going to be very hard, so prepare yourself." Doctors kept saying this, but is there any way really to prepare yourself for your child's death? I hung up the phone and refused to imagine what this might look like.

I was reluctant to give Haven prescription pain medication, knowing it would bury her personality. She would be with us, but not really with us. Also, the need for such medicine meant a miracle hadn't happened and signaled the beginning of the end.

I knew that without God's miraculous intervention, my time with Haven was ticking away. Naturally I questioned why. *Am I not doing enough? Is my faith wavering? Do I have unbelief?* My thoughts volleyed between encouraging myself to continue waiting in faith and accusing myself of not doing enough to move God into action.

WHAT WE BELIEVE ABOUT GOD

We all have a theology, what we believe to be true about God—how good He is, how He operates, what His motives are, what His character is like. And even the best theology is fallible in some way because it is impossible for us human beings to grasp the fullness of the wisdom, love, and grace that God embodies. But we can try. We can make our best attempt. And we should, because what we believe about God informs the way we approach and relate to Him. A healthy theology will direct us to victory and a closer relationship with Christ, but an unhealthy one can lead us to mistrust Him.

WE ALL HAVE A THEOLOGY, WHAT WE BELIEVE TO BE TRUE ABOUT GOD.

How do we develop a healthy theology? Books and sermons and the advice of others can be helpful, but what is most important is spending time in the Word and listening to what the Holy Spirit is speaking to our hearts. Everything we need to know about God's character can be found in His Word; His actions will never deviate from what's written there. And listening to the Spirit is key to understanding the Word. If what we hear is contradictory to what God's Word says about Him, then it isn't from the Lord.

If at all possible, we need to know what we believe about God's character before we are faced with a life crisis. Times of pain are when you should lean on your theology, not create it. But pain will also sift and test what we believe.

For instance, my theology of God had always been that He was good, powerful, able, and eager to bless me. But as I prayed without ceasing and my situation remained unmoved, it challenged what I believed to be true. Was God all these things when it seemed He was withholding good from me? Did He want to bless me simply because I was His daughter or only when I jumped through enough hoops for Him? I was so focused on my expectations being met that I questioned if I was doing things right. I still believed He was good, but I wondered if there was more I needed to do.

Over time, my unmet expectations began to refine the simplistic and perhaps even dogmatic view I had of the way God works. If I served the God who heals, I felt I should be immediately healed. If I served the God who blesses, I should always have more than enough. If I served the God who doesn't disappoint, I should never be disappointed. I might not have admitted these were my expectations of God, but somewhere inside I formed *immediate*, *always*, and *never* in my theology.

But through my trials I've learned that I don't have God all figured out, that He's much more mysterious than I will ever comprehend. Sometimes He chooses to wait instead of giving what we ask *immediately*. Instead of *always* doing what we want, He chooses to act according to His will. And He may allow something we *never* thought He would in order to grow us. As my view of Him has expanded, so have my honor and awe. The God who can't be fit into our mental boxes has inspired me to trust His ways that can't be understood.

Difficult or painful times will expand our concept of God and change our expectations of Him. This is good and healthy. But it should happen only within the parameters of His Word, never outside it.

You won't find any account of Jesus asking those who needed healing to follow certain methods or jump through specific hoops in order to receive their miracle. Instead you'll find Him asking, *Do you believe? What do you want? Do you have faith? Even a small amount will do.* Their miracle was contingent upon their belief in Him and His ability to heal. The bottom line was, did they trust Him to be God? Nothing more, nothing less.

DO WE TRUST GOD TO BE GOD?

I think this holds true for our met expectations and our unmet ones as well. Do we trust God to be God? If we do, once we've done our part of obeying Him, we have to leave the outcome in His hands. What He decides, we must choose to believe is best.

The God we serve exceeds anything we can imagine about Him. Leaning into His mystery creates an open door in our hearts for endless possibility. Looking to His borderless power allows God to frame our thinking and our expectations instead of letting our present circumstances squash and minimize them. I want to always base my life on the limitless power and possibility of God, not on my circumstances.

LESSONS FROM DESPERATION

As the months passed and Haven grew sicker and sicker, I created different narratives as to why God wasn't healing her. Maybe the hold-up was on me. Maybe there was more I needed to learn. *Is God waiting for me to pass a series of faith tests? That must be it. He's teaching me a lesson on how to have more faith.*

I do believe God teaches us through need how to stretch our faith. And I do think that sometimes we are the reason for a delay in God's action. He may be waiting on our obedience or tenderly healing soul wounds before we can move further. But in this instance, though I had not been perfect, I had honestly given Him all that I could. And still it seemed as if He were dangling healing that I wouldn't taste until I moved successfully through the obstacles.

I was desperate for Haven to live. And desperation can be an effective tool to bring our theology to light. In times of desperation we discover if what we profess we believe and what we actually believe are one and the same. Hidden chinks in our theology will reveal themselves as mine did because when our expectations aren't met, we usually blame God for unfaithful character or turn inward and blame ourselves for imperfection.

Again, we all have some inaccurate views of God. Our souls, like our bodies, are living organisms, constantly growing and changing. The closer we get to Christ, the more our understanding of Him should reflect who He really is, but because we are human and fallible, our ideas are too.

Looking back on those desperate days after we brought Haven home, I can see some of my flawed theology at work. I professed that God was good and wanted to heal, but instead of trusting His goodness to do what is right in His eyes, I was really operating from a works mentality to get Him to do what was right in my eyes.

Let me give you an example. Haven had had a Hickman surgically implanted in her chest at the start of her chemotherapy treatments. The port made drawing blood and administering medication easier because it eliminated the need to insert an IV each time. But when she contracted a blood infection, the doctors suggested it had started in her line and recommended that it be permanently removed.

Haven was no longer undergoing chemotherapy treatments and technically didn't need the line, but the idea of removing it was frightening to me. The weaker she became, I thought, the harder it would be to find veins large enough for an IV when she needed care.

After consideration, Casey and I gave the doctors consent to remove the line—because it needed to be done for her health, but also because we decided that it was a faith test. The removal of the Hickman would prove to God that we trusted Him more than anything else.

Looking back, I believe it did take faith to trust God that He would take care of Haven without a line. But while I know our hearts honored Him in this decision, I see now that God was never testing us in this area. In this case, our desperation was warping our view of what God wanted from us.

Desperation that propels us toward God can be a beautiful thing. It can be the catalyst for needed change. But if it simply drives us to work harder, push harder, and prove ourselves to God, it is evidence of a works mentality birthed from fear. A works mentality means we believe deep down that our good works are what make God love us.

Such fear can make us feel like unloved orphans or servants instead of beloved children. But there are no orphans in God's kingdom. Each of us belongs in His house. As Christ followers, each of us has a room with our name on it. Nothing we do or don't do can alter that reality. And when we try, when we let our desperation skew our understanding of how God sees us, we can miss out on experiencing the fullness of His love for us.

I believe that is what happened with us during that frightening episode. We pushed through like strong little faith-soldiers instead of allowing what we really needed, comfort. We should have taken the time to grieve the situation, receive comfort from the Holy Spirit, and gather ourselves to stay our course of faith over the coming months. If we had done that, I believe God would have affirmed that He was indeed taking care of Haven, and we would have been able to live with more peace.

The end result would have been the same. The Hickman would have been removed. The progression of Haven's disease would have continued. It is important that we understand this, but the core belief that motivated our decision would have been healthier, closer to what Scripture tells us about living from a place of grace instead of works. Instead of receiving love and affirmation from God, which is the ultimate act of trust, we gave Him our works, which were motivated by the fear that we weren't doing enough.

I can't help but think of two sisters in the New Testament, Mary and Martha. One worked hard in the kitchen, distracted from Jesus by need, while the other sat at His feet, loving, listening, and learning. Too often I am Martha, working hard to prove my worth, when Jesus wants me to be Mary, resting close to His chest and learning my worth from Him. He wants me to live as a daughter instead of an orphan or a servant. You are God's beloved child. No matter what negative words have been spoken over you. No matter how your pain has tried to define you. No matter what you've done right or wrong. Being God's child is your identity, and you can't change who you are at your core.

DANGLED CHEESE

We were blessed with a wealth of support from people who cared about us. From July to October, a family friend whom I affectionately called Mr. Paul visited our house daily, like clockwork. He would linger for hours at a time, encouraging our faith and joining us in prayer over Haven. Friends, family, and pastors I'd label as giants in faith— Larry Stockstill, Rick Bezet, Chris Hodges, and Karen Territo—came weekly, some daily, to join our fight. When the nights were hard and the hours long, they showed up faithfully. Not only did Karen feed encouragement to my soul, every Friday she fed my junk-food cravings with Raising Cane's chicken strips and fries.

I can't imagine how much harder life would have been without their support. We leaned on them, learned from them, cried with them, and laughed with them. And because of them, I didn't feel alone. Often I'd look through my window blinds and see women walking around my house praying. They'd get back into their cars and drive away without needing recognition. I am forever indebted to the body of Christ for all the love and support that kept me going through those traumatic months.

Even with all this prayer agreement, Haven's health steadily regressed. And through every difficult day, I strived not to waver in unbelief. Scriptures scribbled on pieces of paper lined our bedroom walls. My hands were rarely found without a Bible. Worship music played around the clock. We fasted regularly—at one point, every other day. Sleep was a rare commodity. We were exhausted physically, mentally, and emotionally.

I see now—though I did not see it then—that the pressure to have perfect faith pressed down heavy on my shoulders in those days. Unknowingly I was wearing myself out in a faith-based rat race.

A rat race is an "endless, self-defeating, or pointless pursuit."[1] The phrase equates humans to rodents competing to earn a reward, such as a piece of cheese, but never really getting anywhere. And we do something similar when we wear ourselves out trying to earn an answer to our prayers.

The closer we get to Christ, the more we realize that faith overflows from an intimate relationship with Him. In that relationship, we learn that we cannot earn answers to prayer or manipulate God into giving us what we want or think we need. God's gifts are given freely to those who ask, only according to His good purposes and in His perfect timing. Our good works will never manipulate the will of God.

We receive Christ as our Savior through our faith and His grace.

At that moment we realize the extent of our sin and accept that there's nothing we can do to earn our forgiveness; we can only accept it with gratitude. We choose to believe, in faith, that by some scandalous act of love, God gives grace as a free gift. And it is by faith and grace that we are meant to operate in every area for the rest of our lives. Everything must be filtered through our belief in God and His undeserved favor.

Don't get caught in the rat race trying to earn answers to your prayers. God doesn't dangle cheese. Instead He woos us to Him through relationship. Believe God by taking Him at His word, and leave the outcome to Him.

GETTING BACK IN BALANCE

I've found there are two things with which we struggle most: fear and shame. Fear that God can't. (*My problem is too big, too complicated. Can God really defy her cancer?*) Fear that God won't. (*I know He can, but will He?*) And fear that we're not doing enough. (*Do my righteous works secure my desired outcome?*) Fear is a nasty enemy that doesn't fight fair and breeds toxicity. It pushes us to take matters into our own hands instead of waiting on the will and timing of God.

And then there's shame, which is equally if not more debilitating. Shame makes us believe we're unworthy of God's favor and attention because we're innately lacking or broken. (*I'm damaged goods. I'm not pleasing enough. My insufficiencies are inexcusable to God.*)

Shame discourages conversation. It demands to speak and expects us to listen. And shame isn't reasonable; it's accusing. (*God knows what kind of person you are. He sees right through you. No wonder He doesn't listen to your prayers.*)

Shame steals grace, making it appear scarce, as if God's coveted love pie only has a few crumbs left. We reason that crumbs are better than nothing, so we fight for the morsels, ashamed, yet unwilling to be denied His love. Fight, manipulate, strive, work hard—whatever sacrifice God wants, we'll give Him, because to be left empty would just reinforce our gut-level sense of being unworthy.

Fear and shame don't sit dormant in our hearts' soil like buried bulbs in the winter. They claw and fight for the surface like weeds in springtime. Instead of leading us to God in a healthy way, they push us toward imbalance. Burdened by the heavy yoke of stress and anxiety, we keep trying harder and giving more. And though our specific efforts—prayer, fasting, Bible study, good works—may be very good things, they can be a problem if we're doing them to manipulate God into thinking better of us or granting us the miracles we desire. Then we're setting ourselves up for disappointment because God does not work that way. All that hard work won't change a thing except perhaps to make us bitter or simply wear us out.

I didn't notice I was operating this way. Most of us don't. All I sensed was a desperate fear that I might not get what I thought I couldn't live without. So I made the desired outcome of my situation my own hefty burden to carry. Unknowingly, through fear, I kept trying to step into God's shoes because He wasn't moving quick enough.

Again, none of this was obvious. It was a matter of subtle nuances that revealed a slightly contorted belief system. My thinking was just a few degrees off, but a few degrees of distortion in a foundation can make a tower lean.

I never realized the gaps and imbalances in my theology until my desperate need of God's intervention shined light through the cracks. Thanks be to God that He doesn't leave us the way we are. He reveals so we can be healed. The things He shows us in our hearts that need correction are never to shame us. It is always for the purpose of healing. We are safe in His presence.

Picture a shepherd daily combing his hands over his sheep's coat, checking for any foreign object that might have gotten caught. A briar, for instance, over time, could burrow its way into the sheep's flesh, causing infection. In the same way, God, our Good Shepherd, keeps His hands gently on our hearts, guiding and convicting us of things that will infect our souls. When I realized I had a "lean" in my thinking about God, I asked Him to heal the broken areas He brought to light. Over time He's helped me hone a theology that is closer to His true character.

What I learned through our ordeal with Haven and afterward was that my focus was on my faith more than on God's faithfulness and was constructed on the belief that receiving a miracle was my responsibility.

It's true that our faith opens the door to miracles. And yes, God is waiting for us to ask for what we need and to believe He is able. But that's not what I'm referring to. By "responsibility," I mean an underlying pressure for perfect performance. The assumption that God will draw back His hand of blessing if we mess up too many times.

When our theology tilts in that direction, our obedience to God results partly from a fear of rejection or failure rather than an overflow of love for Him. That's not to say we shouldn't obey Him. But healthy obedience is a by-product of honor and love, and it's born out of intimacy, not fear and shame.

Another way to look at this is to consider the difference between the letter of the law and the spirit of the law. The letter of the law is perfect works and self-righteousness.

HEALTHY OBEDIENCE IS A BY-PRODUCT OF HONOR AND LOVE, AND IT'S BORN OUT OF INTIMACY, NOT FEAR AND SHAME.

The spirit of the law is love and grace. And in a balanced, healthy theology, the spirit trumps the letter every time.

True faith does not reveal itself through works of perfection, but through abiding in God. A habit of time in His presence reveals to us how deep His love is and how able His power is. In time, through the working of the Holy Spirit and the surrender of our will to His, this relationship transforms us. His desires become our own. Our goals get in sync with His plan. We will still do the work of faith, but this time we'll do it out of love.

THE FINE LINE

We always need to factor our humanity into our theology. Meaning, because we're human, there are things we'll get wrong about God. Even those Jesus chose to walk beside Him for three years, privy to insider information about His teaching, often didn't get things right.

WE ALWAYS NEED TO FACTOR OUR HUMANITY INTO OUR THEOLOGY.

In storms they panicked, certain of sure death. Standing next to the Creator, they feared His creation. They witnessed blind men receiving sight but still struggled to believe Jesus could multiply fish and bread.

They were fallible people. Human. So are we. If we expect perfection from ourselves, our humanity will condemn us every time. And if we are looking for a heart completely free of doubt, we will almost certainly be disappointed.

We also need to remember that God can actually use our failures to teach us. Sometimes faith is forged in wrestling with doubt, built in the times we ask for answers and don't hear them, when we seek miracles and don't find them. Our trials can be a gift if we learn from them that faith isn't contingent on our own righteousness or persuading God to do our will, but on our imperfect humanity trusting the righteousness and wisdom of God.

Exhausting ourselves by taking on undue pressure to ensure a miracle is not what God had in mind when He told us to fight the good fight of faith. The fight is good not because we're great warriors, but because we're on the winning side. Victory is ours because of Christ's work. But His burden on us is supposed to be easy, His yoke light (Matt. 11:30). He doesn't set heavy weights upon our shoulders.

God will not be angry with us if we struggle with fear, shame, or doubt or if we fall into the trap of using our works as leverage for His favor. He will simply take us on a journey of learning and finding freedom. And because God wastes nothing, He'll use everything we give Him—even imbalance, error, and struggle—to teach us to trust Him in difficulty and hold tight when He tarries.

All that may leave you with questions. I struggle with them too. At what point do I sign a DNR on my dreams? How can I tell if my request has become an idol? Am I more focused on getting my needs met than on listening to God's heart about it? Do I continue asking God for something I need or want? Do I release my request and assume that what I was asking for wasn't the will of the Lord? Do I continue believing but search for fault in someone, usually myself, as the reason for delay?

It can be hard to locate the fine line between faith and surrender. To start, it's important to recognize that surrender isn't a whatever-God-wants-He's-going-to-get mentality. If God's will in heaven is always done on earth, then why even pray for things? But a dogmatic approach that leaves no room for learning and demands that

IT CAN BE HARD TO LOCATE THE FINE LINE BETWEEN FAITH AND SURRENDER.

God not deny us doesn't change things either. What kind of relationship would we have with Jesus if we assume we must beg and plead to be answered—or that He must automatically give us what we want?

So what is the answer? How do you balance your heart in difficult situations? I don't have a perfect answer. I am a student learning at the feet of Jesus alongside you. But God showed me His heart in the most breathtaking way minutes after we gave Haven her first dose of prescription pain medication. I will never be the same as a result of that one encounter.

A Tender Touch

A plain white paper bag stood erect on the well-worn surface of my hand-me-down kitchen table. All sorts of family secrets shared at dinnertime through the generations are held in the dents and scratches of that wooden surface. The medicine bottle hidden in the bag felt like the enemy. Eyeing it from my chair in the living room, I told myself to keep believing, that God would heal my daughter. Turning my attention to Haven, I saw that her eyes hung heavy and her mouth was turned down. She obviously didn't feel well. She needed the medication.

Now was the time. Casey carried her to our bed and placed her on the right side. My side. After dropping the pink tincture into her mouth, Casey left the room, needing time to process. I lay down next to Haven, propped up on my elbow, speaking soothing words as I watched her body relax.

Within minutes I could see her expression change. Her eyes stared blankly at the white ceiling above as her body stilled. Watching the change should have brought me relief, but instead it felt agonizing. Haven was no longer in pain, and for that I was thankful, but she was also no longer herself. In a sense I had just lost her. Unless God healed her, she would need this medication every four hours and would lie sedated in my bed until the end.

I didn't know how to process this. I wanted to fight, maybe punch a pillow or shake my fist at God; instead I lay quietly and watched the rhythmic way her chest softly rose and fell. My eyes welled up, and a single traitorous tear escaped, trailing slowly down my cheek.

Haven continued to stare blankly at the ceiling. But then suddenly she turned her head and looked at me. Without saying a word, she lifted her hand and touched the tear on my cheek with her index finger. For a split second time stood still.

Then, the moment was over. She put down her finger and stared back up at the ceiling.

I rolled onto my back and sobbed before the Lord. Uncontrollable and unceasing tears drenched my hair and pillow, expressing a mixture of grief and gratitude. I had experienced not only an unforgettable moment between mother and daughter, but also a life-altering exchange between me and my heavenly Father.

I had asked God all day if He saw my pain, if He understood how badly I didn't want this time to come. And He had responded through a delicate touch from her tiny finger. The meaning was tender and supernatural and unmistakable. "I see you, daughter, not just with My eyes, but also with My heart and hands. I am so close I have run My finger down every liquid trail of your pain. I caught that tear. There's not one you've shed that I haven't counted. I see you because I want to—because I love you."

Here on earth there's not a perfect faith formula or an unflawed theology. Imperfection and imbalance will always be with us. But God doesn't require us to be perfect in order to receive His love and attention. He loves us because we are His and because He wants to. Period.

Unfathomable Love

A few years ago I had a dream about my grandfather. Now, I'm from the South, so I knew him as Pawpaw Warren. He was the kindest man to me growing up and had a special way of making me feel loved.

I'm not sure why, but Pawpaw Warren always favored me, and his affirmation helped define my value in my own eyes. "She's a special girl," he'd say to anyone close enough to hear. The sky was my limit in Pawpaw Warren's eyes. Even the horrible sounds I made pecking away on the piano sounded like Mozart to him. Someone probably should have told me the truth about that, but they were all too afraid to cross Pawpaw Warren's favorite girl.

Pawpaw Warren would cook me fried eggs in his cast-iron skillet, then cut the greasy perfection into tiny pieces with his fork and knife like a skilled Samurai. He was a great man in my eyes.

Toward the end of his life, before his short-term memory slipped away, I had the joy of leading my grandfather in a prayer of salvation. Sitting at his kitchen table, we joined hands and I asked him to repeat the prayer after me. That might have been one of the greatest privileges of my life.

Pawpaw Warren had already passed away at the time I dreamed of him, but I am certain God used my grandfather's image as His proxy in that dream. I remember it so vividly. I was walking on the property of my childhood church, and I spotted Pawpaw Warren sitting casually on an old, familiar bridge. I rushed over, happy to see him, and greeted him with a kiss on the lips. He asked me, "What can I do for you?" and I proceeded to tell him that I needed a lavish amount of money for church buildings and orphanages. (Don't think I'm too holy. If it hadn't been a Spirit-led dream, I might have asked for a lavish amount of money for myself!) The next thing I heard was his voice replying, "Oh, unbelieving generation." Then I woke up.

That dream, with its reference to Mark 9:19—where Jesus healed a possessed boy and rebuked His disciples for their lack of faith—shook me. It reminded me that God wants to meet not just my needs but also my desires. Then He lovingly rebuked me for not believing that He could and would. Through it God showed me how much He longs for His children to know that He is waiting to care for us, that all we have to do is ask.

So why didn't God give me the greatest desire of my heart, the healing of my child? I simply don't know. It's hard to fathom the ways of God. I don't pretend to understand them fully. And honestly, I'm thankful for it. To know the ways of God would be to reduce Him to the smallness of my humanity. The God we serve cannot be contained by earthly spaces. He is wildly untamable, and for that I'm grateful. And when I don't understand, that's when I must trust. When it seems that He contradicts His Word, I realize that I don't understand His Word as well as I thought I did, that I have much to learn.

I also suspect that some of the baffling and frightening experiences of that time may have originated with the enemy, not with God.

Only in God's Time

One afternoon Casey left the house for a quick run to the grocery store. I watched the taillights of his Camry travel down our long driveway, and the very second he turned the corner, our electricity went out. That meant the home telephone wasn't working—and neither was the oxygen machine Haven now depended on. Without assisted breathing, she began choking and vomiting.

I didn't know what to do. Casey had the only cell phone we owned with him in the car. I couldn't call him or summon an ambulance for help. One of my worst fears was coming to life. I felt alone and completely helpless, realizing my daughter might die on me right there and I could do nothing about it—except pray. I prayed and prayed and said the name of Jesus over and over.

The power stayed out for thirty minutes and came back on minutes before Casey pulled back into our driveway. I don't think that was a coincidence. I'm convinced that Satan tries to create situations to make us think that we've done something wrong, that God isn't happy with us or that He's choosing to test us. I don't believe that particular afternoon was some cruel test designed by God. I think Satan wanted to shake me and, in my fear, tempt me to turn in anger toward the Lord. I don't know all that was going on behind the scenes, but I do know that while Haven struggled for those thirty minutes, God was with us and sovereign over the situation. Haven was not going to perish until He said it was time. And I wasn't going to lose myself if I was next to Him.

What we think is cruelty on God's part may in fact be from Satan. But God is God and will never let us be destroyed, neither by His trials and tests nor by our enemy's schemes.

DARK DAYS

Haven continued to decline daily, and her needs intensified to the point that she now needed around-the-clock care. Periodically a hospice nurse would visit our home and offer support, but Casey and I were the primary caregivers.

We continued to worship, pray, and believe for a miracle. And we felt God's nearness intensely. Some of my fondest memories of the presence of God center around that time. Like feeling empowered even on the hardest of days, or the tender moments He comforted me in worship when I felt as if I couldn't continue, or the phone calls from friends when I needed them most, or a timely scripture of encouragement to show me that He hears me, sees me, and will never leave me.

Even when I was frustrated with God because I felt He could have changed my scenario and stopped Haven's suffering, I still felt Him close. He didn't leave me to do the hard things alone. And even when I disagreed with His choices, instead of pushing me away, He'd wrap me in His big arms and tug me in close to His chest to feel His heartbeat.

It had been five months since we moved home from Memphis—five incredibly long and arduous months that were far more difficult than the doctors had warned they'd be. God's sustaining grace for each day enabled me to endure more than I ever thought possible. I experienced disappointment and fear, but by the grace of God, I continued following the dark and unknown path where He led me.

The only illumination along the way came from the internal hope the Holy Spirit gave me each day—not just hope that Haven could still be healed, but hope that no matter what I went through, I could not be separated from His love. He had proven that to me many times over the previous ten months.

The air outside was crisp with a slight October chill, and the leaves had started to wither in surrender to fall. The comforting smells and sounds of autumn drifted in the air—the clean scent of cooler air, the rustling of the wind through the trees. This was all so familiar, yet this October was unlike any other I had ever experienced.

Haven had been immobile in our bed on pain medication for more than eight weeks. Every few days her body weight seemed to drop, and she no longer resembled my little girl. The last time the hospice nurse had weighed her—three weeks earlier—she'd tipped the scales at a mere seven pounds, weighing the same at twenty-one months old as she had weighed at birth.

If there was hell on earth, then I smelled the singed hairs on my arm and my clothes reeked of smoke. Every day it grew harder to watch Haven suffer. My heart had long ago melted into puddles of pain. Every measure we had taken to make her better had failed. I had nothing left, no hope except for Jesus. He was the only thing I could cling to.

Countless times I lay prostrate on my bedroom floor, face to the carpet, confessing healing over Haven. Often my prayers would turn from professions of faith into begging God to do what I asked and then back to faith. I must have said the words *I believe* and *please* ten thousand times and in every combination imaginable. "I believe Haven is healed. God, I believe You can heal her. Please heal her. Please do this for me. Please, I'm begging You not to let me lose her. Please stop this. Please, please, please, God." It was an intense time of spiritual warfare, not only for Haven's body but for my own heart to continue trusting the Lord.

LETTING GO

It was the nineteenth of October. The time was ten twenty-five at night. The hum of the oxygen machine droned on in our bedroom. I noticed a change in my daughter's blank expression and felt an urgency to hold her. This wasn't something we did often because moving caused her discomfort.

Casey carefully laid Haven's tiny body on a pillow in my lap as I sat in a rocking chair. I could tell she was fighting for life. All I wanted to do in that moment was tell her I loved her. Over and over I told her. My mother heart had already been pulverized into tiny pieces, and I didn't know how much more it could take.

Finally I said the most honest prayer I could formulate with words. It was risky and desperate. I sat as still as I could, careful not to jostle her. I spoke no truer words than these: "God, we've given You every opportunity to heal Haven. I've given it all I have. I have no regrets because I know I have believed You as best as I know how. I have fought the good fight of faith. But Jesus, I can't stand to watch the suffering any longer. My heart hurts, but I release Haven to You. If You're not going to heal her, as hard as this is to say, please take her now."

An exhale of relief escaped from my lungs as I surrendered my will to God. I let go—not of His ability to heal my daughter, but of what I wanted. For the first time I released the outcome to Him. Ten months of intense spiritual warfare, joy and pain, light and darkness, death and life, heaven and hell culminated in this one moment. Haven was in His hands. Whether she lived or died was His to decide.

Two minutes later she exhaled her last breath in my arms.

EIGHT

DEALING WITH DISAPPOINTMENT

Faith does not eliminate questions. But
faith knows where to take them.
Elisabeth Elliot

Two thousand pairs of eyes settled on Casey and me the morning
of Haven's funeral. I noticed the stolen glances and inquisitive looks,
and it made me feel the need to carefully measure my expressions.
Many of these people had walked closely with us through the previous ten months. They, too, had invested countless hours praying and
believing God for Haven's healing, so our loss was their loss.

I could see in their faces the same unresolved questions that Casey
and I were struggling with:

Why does God let bad things happen?

Does He still heal today?

How do I feel about a God who didn't do what He says in His Word
He will do?

Now they seemed to wait with bated breath for how we would

respond to our unwanted outcome—to God not doing what we had asked Him to do.

I'd like to be able to say that my response was honest and vulnerable, and perhaps it was as authentic as I could manage at the time. But even as I smiled bravely, I noticed my smile was too big, too forced. My words seemed too calculated, my eyes too dry.

To everyone else my resolute smile communicated that I was at peace with God's decision to take Haven. I even tried hard to convince myself I felt that way. I focused more on comforting those around me than on allowing them to comfort me.

Sometimes life is so overwhelming in the moment that we need a substantial amount of time to pass to be able to accurately look back and judge our hearts. Only a lot of reflection and the willingness to grow eventually unearthed the hidden issues I was dealing with that day. Just forty-eight hours away from Haven's death, I hadn't yet had the time to process why I was so driven to be strong. Much later I came to realize that it was in part a cover-up for the disappointment I was hiding not only from the world but also from myself.

A PATTERN OF DISAPPOINTMENT

Recently I had a conversation with friends about their times of disappointment with God. Sarah's twins were born with Down syndrome. Kelly struggles with infertility while her heart's cry is to hold a child of her own in her arms. Jennifer had dreams of a good marriage, but it's a year after their wedding, and they barely get along.

I noticed a pattern in all their stories. Every woman said it took her a while to search her heart with honesty and admit to herself that she was disappointed not only with her circumstances but with God.

And each one attributed her reluctance to acknowledge the truth to two reasons: (1) not having answers to questions that surfaced because God didn't meet her expectations, and (2) not wanting to disappoint Him with her frustration, confusion, and discouragement. Their brave words echoed my heart's experience with Haven.

We've already touched on the subject of disappointments in this book, but now I want to focus a whole chapter on them. And I don't mean those everyday letdowns or Chick-fil-A forgetting your waffle fries in the drive-through. (Although eating your chicken sandwich with no fries can be pretty devastating, it's not life altering.) I mean the bone-aching, heart-crushing, makes-you-feel-forgotten-and-rejected kind of disappointments we experienced when we prayed until our voices gave out and nothing changed. When we did all we could do and it wasn't enough. When our high hopes have been dashed low, when the sky falls and the ground shakes.

That kind of disappointment is hard to navigate, perhaps because we never seem to see it coming. It's like that car accident I mentioned back in chapter 1, the one that happened in high school. All I remember is crossing an intersection, then feeling a sudden impact and spinning across two lanes. I never even saw the other car.

We're tempted to bury this kind of disappointment because we're uncomfortable, and there are a variety of reasons for this discomfort.

There is shame: "I shouldn't feel this way. It's unchristian."

There is fear: "Won't God be mad at me?"

There is isolation: "I'm the only one feeling this way."

There is denial: "If I don't admit it, my perfect picture of God will stay intact."

In my case, I think I may have been trying to shield myself, others, and even God Himself from some of the unresolved questions in my heart and head. Coming to recognize this was a weighty revelation.

I saw a woman who was protecting herself from being crushed under the gravity of her disappointment. A woman protecting the world from seeing a God who, for reasons only known to Him, doesn't always do what we expect Him to do. And a woman protecting God from her unresolved questions for fear they may be hurtful or offensive to Him.

Sitting with this, I also realized that most of my life I had striven to protect the narrative of God that I wanted myself and others to know. This is mostly what drove me to put on a brave face. I feared that if I unearthed my disappointment, the pure and perfect picture of the God I wanted the world to see would be marred.

> **GOD DOESN'T ALWAYS PLAY BY OUR RULES. AND HE HAS EVERY RIGHT NOT TO BECAUSE HE IS GOD.**

I needed this perfect image of God because it made me feel secure. But how secure are we, really, with a facade? A fabricated picture is no picture at all. Putting our trust in a fairy-tale version of God only causes more insecurity.

As I've thought about this over the years and talked to others, I've decided that our personal theologies often don't hold space for these scenarios where God doesn't meet our expectations. Too often, in hopes of finding some assurance in the uncertainty of life, we attempt to force-fit the God of the universe into tidy boxes small enough for our finite minds to comprehend. We attempt to domesticate God—to make Him tamer, more predictable, more obedient to our desires. We want Him in bite-size pieces we can chew. But doing this strips away the very mystery and wonder that make Him God and that bring us security and peace.

What gives us confidence can also be what scares us. What keeps us in awe can also be what we want to tame. God doesn't always play by our rules. And He has every right not to because He is God.

PINHOLES IN THE PICTURE

Everyone at the funeral knew that for ten months we had made a stand to believe God for Haven's healing. We'd put everything we possessed mentally, physically, and emotionally into the spiritual battle for her healing. And yet she had lost the fight. Casey and I had lost the fight. Everyone who believed with us had lost this fight with cancer.

From the beginning, I understood that my daughter's death was inevitable without a miracle, but I wasn't expecting her to die. Honestly, I'm glad I wasn't expecting it because I would much rather give God room to be the miraculous One He is than to shut down my faith so that my expectations were met. But as her health worsened and the miracle I expected didn't come to pass, tiny pinholes appeared in my ideal picture of a trustworthy God who always fixes the situation, rushes in to save the day, and never lets His children down.

And do you know what? God *does* always fix the situation. He *does* save the day. He *does* never let His children down. But I have learned over time that He does it in His way, His will, and His timing. Jesus has already fixed the situation through the cross. He has saved the day, but it may not show itself in my timing, and though God doesn't always do what I want, He has never once let me down, not in the long term. But the way He does these things often bears little resemblance to the way I pictured it.

When Haven passed away, the picture my expectations had painted was so marred that it barely resembled the God I thought I knew, so I overcompensated in the areas I believed Him to be short. I plugged the pinholes by telling myself to be strong, and I smiled hard. I spoke hope into dozens of bewildered faces. "God has our best interest in mind," I told them.

I never made a calculated decision to do this or even realized in the moment what I was doing. Perhaps I was confessing by faith what I knew to be true even when I didn't feel it; there is definitely a place for that. But I'm convinced my faithful facade also came from a misguided sense of duty that in turn sprang from a misunderstanding of the place of disappointment in our lives.

As I struggled in the wake of Haven's death, I mistakenly viewed my disappointment with God as something wrong, something to fear and to hide, so I masked it.

Now, a mask can be an excellent cover—especially when it looks similar to who you are or who you want to be, only slightly more polished and refined. We may not even be aware we've put a mask like that on. Our motive for wearing it isn't necessarily to be fake or to hide ourselves. Sometimes we just aren't ready to investigate and deal with what's inside our hearts. So we push ourselves, convince ourselves, even, that our hearts are fine. We work hard on our masks, carefully cutting and pasting layers of happiness.

If we're forced into a moment of honesty, we might admit that deep down we are confused, hurt, and possibly starting to become bitter. But this is a scary admission. Most of us haven't been taught what to do with these kinds of feelings, especially toward God, so we keep the mask handy. But we can fool ourselves and others only so long with even the best *God is good* and *I'm doing great* expressions.

Matthew 12:34 says that "out of the abundance of the heart the mouth speaks" (ESV). Just as words are a telling sign of the true nature of the heart, the face also communicates what's veiled within. If the internal and external don't align, when the cameras and crowds look away, the smile will fade and the face will turn downcast.

Maybe that is you. I think it's safe to say it's been all of us at one point or another. Underneath our carefully polished masks, many of our faces are deeply creased with disappointment that no amount of Botox can erase. And eventually our masks will wear thin and crack at the seams. What's inside will demand to be hidden no longer.

The Danger of Hiding Disappointment

Why is it so important to acknowledge our disappointment? Because left to itself its toxicity will fester and spread.

A few years ago my neighbor noticed a faint smell of mildew in her daughter's room, though no signs of mold or moisture showed on the surface. Not knowing what to do, she did what we all do; she crossed her fingers and hoped it would go away on its own. A few weeks later, after her daughter began battling severe allergy-like symptoms, she decided it was time to call in the professionals. After pulling back some of the Sheetrock, they discovered most of the wall had been overtaken with black mold.

These tiny spores aren't dangerous in themselves, but they can release harmful toxins that are hazardous to our health if breathed in over a period of time. In my neighbor's case, doctors believed that the mold was indeed the cause of her daughter's symptoms. Hidden beneath the surface, behind the cheerful painted exterior, the mold was given the perfect conditions to grow.

Disappointment in the soul is like the black mold in my neighbor's house. It grows best when it's concealed and undisturbed, particularly because we don't want to acknowledge it. The longer it goes undealt with, the more it spreads, the harder we must work to hide it, the more we have to lie to ourselves that our hearts are okay, and the more driven we are to say and do all the right things so that others won't see our internal battle.

A heart that is hiding disappointment eventually becomes guarded and distrusting. To *distrust* something or someone means "to regard with doubt and suspicion."[1] And that's a real problem when we begin distrusting God. That kind of doubt is the antithesis of faith. While faith compels us to trust God even when we don't understand Him, doubt prompts us to look inward for answers because God doesn't make sense to us. And unchecked doubt easily gives rise to fear, anger, bitterness, cynicism, resentment, and hopelessness.

A friend of mine recently told me that her teenage son who had been raised in church had renounced God. He told his parents that his experiences in life had led him to conclude that God wasn't real. I couldn't help but wonder what pain this young man had experienced that Satan had distorted and magnified. I wondered if he'd faced disappointment and didn't know what to do with it. Instead of bringing it to God, it's possible he'd felt ashamed and confused and had begun to doubt instead.

Every time our expectations of God and our reality don't align, we make a decision, whether knowingly or unknowingly, about what we believe to be true of Him. When our experience and our theology intersect, we are forced to decide if we will believe God's Word or our experience. Sadly, my friend's son chose to believe the lie entangled in his experience.

HEARTACHE PROVIDES FERTILE GROUND FOR THE ENEMY'S LIES AGAINST GOD TO BE PLANTED AND TO GROW.

What lies does your painful experience tell you? That God is aloof? That God isn't good? That God can't be trusted?

I've found that the more painful the experience, the more lies can appear to be true. Heartache provides fertile ground for the enemy's lies against God to be planted and to grow. It's one of Satan's favorite ways to take advantage of our disappointment.

If we've been rejected, for example, Satan will seize his opportunity to tell us that the rejection was our fault because we're not good enough or smart enough or pretty enough. Of course this is untrue, but it may *feel* true. And if we don't bring it to the Lord to help us sort it all out, we may end up building our beliefs about ourselves and God upon a cracked foundation.

Good counsel should be our ally in the midst of difficult situations. A trusted outside perspective, such as that of a counselor, a pastor, or a wise friend, can shed light on dark lies that we are having difficulty seeing through.

But nothing has come close to the clarity I receive when I hear for myself God's truth about my situation. To detangle from Satan's lies, we need to ask God where He was when our pain happened and what He wants to say to us about it. Then we need to get quiet and listen. If you hear anything contrary to God's Word, throw it out. God's truth will always be reassuring and encouraging. And if we receive His truth, it will correct our thinking and release us from the lies we might be believing.

Disappointment and bitterness are so closely related that it's difficult to recognize when one turns into the other. But if disappointment is left undealt with, it shifts into bitterness quickly. It's a good idea to check our words, our thoughts, and our attitudes, perhaps by asking a trusted friend or family member for input. If we're producing bitter fruit, then we have a tainted root that needs to be dealt with— unearthed, pulled up, brought to the Lord, and possibly discussed with others. What matters most is replacing the lie that caused the disappointment with truth.

I expected healing for Haven, but I experienced her final breath in my arms. A giant chasm packed with life-shattering pain lay between the two. As a result, my heart was fertile ground to believe the lies that God had withheld good from me, that cancer had won, and that God hadn't loved me enough to keep my heart from breaking. Satan planted those seeds in the nucleus of my experience, but allowing them to grow was my choice.

I've seen too many people walk away from God because He didn't do what they wanted Him to do. They faced a crisis that could have turned them to God for answers, but instead they inclined their ear to Satan's convincing interpretation of their pain. It sounds something like, *God must not love you as much as you think He does. Maybe He's not 100 percent good because He could have prevented this, which means there are parts of Him that can't be trusted.*

Our response to disappointment and Satan's lies doesn't have to be as extreme as turning away from Christ or shaking our fists toward heaven to be damaging. It can be as subtle as losing trust. Trust is vital in any relationship, but especially with our Savior. To follow Him forward out of disappointment and into the plans He has for our lives, we have to trust that He will get us there safe and sound.

We might find ourselves wondering how we will trust God in the future because, from where we are now standing, it seems He has failed us in the present. This is when many of us ponder the notion that if we can't fully trust God, then who can we trust?

Me is usually the answer. So we put a white-knuckle grip on life. We snatch the reins, grasp tightly, and attempt to control the narrative because we've believed the lie that says, *I'm the only one I can depend on.* If God is even a fraction of the things Satan accuses Him of being, then He isn't reliable, and we need to protect our hearts like a newborn baby because we're not sure they can handle any more shattering.

NAMING MY DISAPPOINTMENT

The subtle deception of doubt stemming from disappointment may happen overnight or over a long period of time. For me it was a slow burn. After months of struggle with Haven, my picture of God as a safe, loving Father had morphed just slightly. It wasn't a dramatic shift, but enough of one for me to hold my heart a little more protectively. Hiding my disappointment had left an open door. Distrust had wormed its way into my heart without me knowing.

As a result, little by little God started to resemble a stern, tough love–type father who was more concerned with teaching me character than comforting my soul. I believed the character lesson was for my good, but the teaching method felt devoid of care and affection. My mind knew that God loved me. But I felt numb. Maybe it was grief. Maybe disappointment. Maybe a mixture of both. I needed to own up to my disappointment so that it wouldn't morph into bitterness. Instead, I put on my mask and overcompensated.

For several weeks after Haven's funeral I continued on this way—being the protector, wearing my mask, saying the right words, and hiding my disappointment. Then finally, one chilly November afternoon, I decided I was too tired to continue patching the holes in my picture of God. I dared to open the rusting door to my soul and allowed myself to see, and then to admit to God, what was really inside.

I was in our bedroom with Holland, rocking her into an afternoon nap. I swooshed back and forth in a hypnotic rhythm in the same wooden rocking chair where Haven had lain in my arms for the last time.

I had thought once or twice about putting that rocker in the attic so I wouldn't be reminded of that painful night. But then I'd conclude that the chair wasn't the problem. Those memories were stored in every fiber of my being. If I wanted to run away from them, I would have to buy a new house, get rid of my bed, and purge my mind of all things related to the last year. So I kept the chair right next to my side of the bed, where Haven used to lie.

Looking down at Holland as I rocked, all I could see was how much she resembled her older sister. For a brief moment it felt as if I were holding Haven again. Even while my arms held one child, they were bereft of the other. And that barrenness brought up floods of emotions that I had worked tirelessly to avoid. Maybe you haven't lost a child, but I think it's safe to say that we all understand that disappointment brings feelings of emptiness even while holding a blessing.

I was tempted to put Holland in her crib and busy myself with computer work or calling a friend, anything to avoid the moment. But even though I felt so uncomfortable, part of me felt compelled to stay in the place of vulnerability.

I knew that, with God, healing always comes with yielding. So I willed myself to continue sitting in that rocker. And then I sensed the scalpel in His hand. He wanted to repair in me the trust in Him that life had damaged.

"Jesus, do surgery on my heart," I whispered, very aware of the irony of asking God to heal me of my disappointment and distrust of Him. Still, truth told me that asking was safe and that even if His scalpel wounded, it would ultimately heal. In God's hands, extraction doesn't mean subtraction. He cuts away only what is hindering growth so that our hearts will yield abundance.

"I'm devastated," I cried out as the dam broke. "So disappointed in life and in You. My heart hurts in ten thousand ways I didn't know existed."

I had said words like this before, but this time enough days had passed since Haven's death that I was ready to face just how disappointed I really was. Painful as this was, it was also freeing to realize that I didn't have to be strong here in this space. In this sacred moment I wasn't Stacy the leader, Stacy the pastor, or even Stacy the woman who had publicly lost her child with everyone watching her response. I was Stacy the daughter. God didn't expect anything of me, except to be His child in vulnerability and truth.

Still holding Holland, I waited for a reply, something from heaven. All I heard was the swooshing of the rocker. I wondered if my heart's intense ache was arresting my ability to hear what God might have to say. Taking His silence as an open door, I continued on.

"Why didn't You do what I asked You to do? I had faith. I pleaded. I begged. Are You trying to teach me a lesson? Am I so incomplete that I need to learn from something so painful? I cannot comprehend Your decision to take Haven. It makes no sense to me. I'm trying to find worthy reasons for it, but I can't. I'm trying desperately to trust You, but it's so, so hard."

And still silence.

After baring my soul, I pleaded with God to take away the pain. And still I felt it.

God didn't respond in an audible way that day. I didn't have an aha moment where suddenly everything came to light. There was no clear sense of His words in my spirit, as I had experienced in the past. And the pain of loss wasn't suddenly removed; it was as intense as ever. But rocking in that chair, I felt Him in a thick, almost tangible, way. I sensed His love and approval settle on me in that holy space like gentle dew that saturated the dry places in my soul. I wanted to breathe it in, bathe in it, never let it go.

I had dared to remove the protective shell around my broken heart and let it beat freely with disappointment. It was my sincere offering to God, and He received it with grace, as any good father would. He didn't discard my vulnerability like a crumpled piece of waste. There was no correction or rebuke. He simply listened. To every word. And He accepted me as I was, disappointment and all.

That moment of tenderness wooed me to believe that there was more beyond my disappointment. I knew that afternoon that I would breathe once again because I could feel Him leading me forward out of Harran.

That day changed me. It changed my relationship with God. And it left me wondering if what I'd experienced could change things for others too.

What if instead of hiding our disappointment from God, we let it be our offering to Him? Is it possible that our honesty is an aroma rising to heaven that God accepts and calls good? I cannot think of purer worship to the Lord than to lay pretense down at His feet and offer our true selves. By holding nothing back, even our disappointment, by giving Him everything to use for His glory, we are worshiping our Savior in spirit and in truth and also allowing Him access to heal every broken area in our lives. Complete surrender is more pleasing to God than the right answer and a well-formed prayer.

> **WHAT IF INSTEAD OF HIDING OUR DISAPPOINTMENT FROM GOD, WE LET IT BE OUR OFFERING TO HIM?**

GOD KNOWS DISAPPOINTMENT TOO

As I let God in, His tenderness revealed something new to me, however: God knows disappointment too. I had never considered this, but as I shed tears in that rocking chair, it felt as though heaven wept with me.

Perhaps it is a new concept for you to consider that God can be disappointed. However, the reality is that God doesn't get everything

He wants. Second Peter 3:9 tells us that He wills that all people are saved through Jesus, and yet people die every day without receiving Christ. This is not what God wants, but it happens. I think it's fair to say that even though He's sovereign, He's still disappointed by that.

I believe God also grieves over pain and loss, even when He chooses to allow it. Could God have prevented Haven's death? Yes. Did He allow it? Yes. Could He have healed her? Yes. But the same could be said of Jesus. God could have stopped the crucifixion. But He didn't. And the brutality of the lashes Jesus endured on His back for our healing was not experienced in vain—for by those stripes we have been healed (Isa. 53:5).

This is the mystery of God. There are things that He allows in His sovereignty that we may never comprehend while on this side of eternity. But that doesn't mean He doesn't grieve.

My pain was validated when I sensed God's grieving heart with me. Heaven gave weight to my loss. It was as if Jesus spoke to my heart, *I am personally acquainted with your sorrow.*

His love and approval were like tender whispers of truth from the Holy Spirit:

I'm sorry you're hurting.

I love you more deeply than you'll ever know.

I promise I am already redeeming this for your good and for the enemy's demise. You'll see.

I knew that day as I rocked Holland that the source of my healing would be the love and truth I heard in my encounters with God. I realized that His image never needed protecting, that He was complete and perfect in Himself, and that He fiercely loves His children and is devoted to bringing good from what Satan meant for harm. When I realized that, I committed to be as vulnerable as possible with Him.

My situation didn't change that afternoon in the rocker. Haven was still gone, and I was still grieving, but my heart felt lighter. Opening my soul to trust God guided me to be able to see my heartache as a crossroads on the way to His promises and to continue down the pathway of healing instead of planting my feet in disappointment.

HE MADE US. HE KNOWS HOW TO HEAL US.

God won't ask us to fight our way to healing. But He does ask us to yield a vulnerable heart and let His words foster recovery. Psalm 55:22 offers this: "Give all your cares to the Lord and He will give you strength. He will never let those who are right with Him be shaken" (NLV).

Most of my healing since that day has come through encounters I had in God's presence—in worship, in honest conversation, and in those beautiful times while reading Scripture when the Word came alive, jumped off the page, and infiltrated and healed areas of my heart. Without such God encounters, I would have been left to heal by nothing but human methods of self-help. These can be beneficial, but they will not heal as deeply as God's Spirit can and will. Many of our hurts are built on lies that only God's truth can reveal. There are some pains that only His touch can mend. He made us. He knows how to heal us.

I wonder how many hurting people are stuck at a dead end and don't see a way out because they haven't completely opened themselves up to God. I know it's not easy; vulnerability doesn't always come naturally for me either. When my child was ripped from my arms and the ache was so strong it tore open the raw flesh of my heart, the pain felt so sacred I wanted to guard it with my life. Exposing it before God was the most vulnerable thing I had ever done.

My hesitancy to reveal my disappointment made me wonder if maybe I wasn't ready to let go of it. Did it somehow validate the hell I had been through? Was I protecting it instead of protecting my heart from it?

I had to admit I had become almost comfortable in my pain.

Familiar with it. Nearly on the verge of settling down, buying a house together, and picking out curtains for the windows. And I was scared to release it because that might mean I somehow approved of Haven's death. Life had done me wrong, and letting go seemed like I was letting life off the hook.

But let's be honest. When we speak of "life," sometimes we mean God. We think that God has done us wrong and that letting go of disappointment means letting God off the hook. When I realized that about myself, that's when I started to realize I may have valued my disappointment more than my freedom.

The Case for Moving Forward

A year after Haven's death, I admitted to Casey that I was having a hard time moving forward. I felt guilty but was afraid to surrender my pain. And though I knew this was all a natural part of grief, I felt stuck. But Casey said something that cut the strings that bound me. He reminded me of the time that King David fasted for his sick child to be healed. After much prayer, the child died. David knew that nothing else could be done. So, accepting God's decision, he bathed, got dressed, and ate (2 Sam. 12:15–22).

Reading between the lines, I don't think David pushed his grief into the past and "got over it." I think it's safe to say that his tears mingled with his dinner that night. And yet he chose to move forward.

For each of us, forward takes a different amount of time. But forward is the only place worth going.

Moving on with life is not irreverent. It's not disrespectful. It's not letting life off the hook or saying that what happened is okay. We're acknowledging that the person hurt us or the situation confused us or the outcome shattered our dreams, but that in spite of all of it we're following Jesus. Which is about the most reverent thing you can do.

We won't move forward, however, unless we're ready to deal with our disappointment. Until then we're still on our faces, fasting for something that's already been decided.

If we want to move forward toward the promises of God that await us, we have to get honest with God and ourselves. Vulnerability is what will open our hearts' doors to heaven's leading. It's the oxygen that gives life to our journey with God. It turns our tragic dead ends into hopeful crossroads.

The very nature of vulnerability exposes the true you—not the church you or the person you wish to be, but the real you, in all of your fears and inadequacies. It means taking a chance that this person will be loved and protected by God. It means having faith that God will place something far more worthy and valuable in your open hands than what you release to Him.

God wants to repair our trust in Him that life has damaged. If we insist on holding our cards close to our chests and protecting ourselves from God, we will be missing connection with our Healer. Surrendering all—bitterness, anger, pain, confusion, whatever causes us to remain protective—is what propels us toward health.

The road of trust and vulnerability may look frightening and unfamiliar. But as we surrender all and commit our steps to Christ, we learn that it's an even path, paved and smoothed with stability. And as we continue to travel, we'll get a glimpse of newness on the horizon.

It starts as a tiny sliver of light. But the more we step toward it, the bigger it gets. Our feet start feeling lighter. The hindrances fall off and litter the path behind us.

Why would we retreat to our hiding places when we can see the promise up ahead?

NINE

EVEN WHEN HE DOESN'T FEEL GOOD

My brother-in-law Buck followed the same routine every morning. He walked a mile for exercise on his two hundred acres. But this particular morning was different. On the last leg of his usual trail, he rounded the corner to walk the strip that ran along the country road bordering his property. A car slowed and came to a stop beside him. The window rolled down, and the nose of a shotgun poked out. Before Buck could respond, the mysterious driver pulled the trigger and shot him. Shrapnel pierced his flesh as he fell to the ground. Realizing he was still alive, the gunman shot a second time, then rolled up the window and sped away. Miraculously, Buck survived the episode, but the crazed gunman went on a series of four such shooting sprees, claiming the lives of three men.

When Casey and I received the phone call that Buck had been shot but was alive, we stopped what we were doing and praised God profusely for being so good as to spare his life. If Buck had been killed, the effect on our family would have been devastating. Buck has three kids and a wife who can't imagine life without him. Losing him would have been incredibly tough for all of us. We were grateful that God had been so good and gracious to our family. But what about the families of the three men who lost their lives because of this deranged man's actions? Was God good to them? Was He just interested in saving Buck but not the other three?

One of the most pervasive questions about God is "Is He good?" If we google those words, more than two hundred million results instantly pop up. If we google "Why does God let bad things happen?" we'll find just as many opinions.

People ask these questions because life is not simply a collection of numbered days. It's a compilation of experiences that we feel, touch, taste, smell, and see. And life, to be honest, doesn't always look or feel good. Often it brings us physical or mental or emotional pain. And when that happens, we can't simply ignore the experience. We have to deal with it in some way.

This is simply the way life works. But if we bring God into the picture—which He already is, of course—the questions become inevitable. Would a good God allow me or anyone else to hurt?

What the Bible Says

God is good all the time. We are taught that in churches, books, songs, and podcasts. If we grow up in a Christian home, we learn it before we can read, and most Christians would claim to believe it. And Scripture enthusiastically proclaims God's goodness. Numerous verses in the Old Testament invite us to give thanks:

> Give thanks to the LORD, for he is good;
> his love endures forever.
>
> (1 Chron. 16:34; Ps. 106:1; 107:1)

Both Old and New Testament describe Him with words meaning beneficial, pleasant, agreeable, and kind, and both ascribe to Him a kind of moral excellence or piety.[1]

When referring to God in Scripture, *good* is both a noun and an adjective, nature and attribute. It's who He is and what He does. His good deeds flow from His good nature. His creation is good (Gen. 1; 1 Tim. 4:4). His words are good (Ps. 119:103). He works everything together for good (Rom. 8:28).

And the Bible tells us that God is not only good, but that He is also good to us (Ps. 31:19; Matt. 7:11; James 1:17). God and goodness are synonymous. We can't have God without goodness. If we took God out of this world, there would be no goodness.

We may claim to believe it, and many of us do. But when real life happens, I wonder how often that phrase actually goes beyond words to conviction in our human hearts. I also wonder how often life leads us to question, even just a little, our good-God theology.

The Psalms, especially, are full of tributes to God's essential goodness. Psalm 34:8, for example, invites us to "taste and see that the LORD is good." When we experience God, the implication is that we'll find His goodness is like honey or chocolate; it motivates us to keep coming back for more. The more we "taste" of Him, the easier we'll find it to trust Him, because each "bite" will be better than the previous one.

THE PROBLEM WITH EXPERIENCE

Practically speaking, though, relying on our experience alone to understand God's goodness can be problematic, because our experience is limited and our point of view is inevitably biased. If we try to derive our understanding from the circumstances of our lives, then our view of God's goodness will change with those circumstances. We may assume that God is good when life is good. But when life is bad, is God bad or only partly good?

Let's go back to Buck for a moment. Three other men lost their lives. While I'm thanking God's goodness for protecting Buck, someone else may be blaming Him for not protecting *their* brother-in-law. Which one of us is right? Is God good or is He not?

If we are judging God's nature according to circumstance, my instincts would say both families are right. God is good because He protected one and bad because He didn't protect the other. But God cannot be judged that way. Circumstances can't define or change who He is. If Scripture says that God is good, then He is good in action, word, and thought. He is perfect in every way.

So how do we reconcile the apparent gap between God's goodness and our experience of pain? How does it fit in our theology? Can we say God is good in hard times as easily as we say it in blessed times?

I won't attempt to explain why the Lord allows bad things to happen. Honestly, I don't know. And I believe that those who give us trite, oversimplified, unsatisfactory answers to this question usually do so in an effort to make the subject more understandable or palatable.

Let's be honest: not everything about God is naturally palatable to our taste. I don't like that children perished in the Genesis flood or that Job suffered and wasn't given a reason why or that God allowed His innocent Son to die or that Paul had a trial that God never removed or that John was exiled on an island for his beliefs. I don't like these things because I can't understand why a good God would allow them. But God had a divine purpose for all of them, one that was good, right, and holy.

In C. S. Lewis's novel *The Lion, the Witch and the Wardrobe*, there is a scene that gives us a good start in reconciling this puzzling dilemma. It takes place between the girl Susan and a talking beaver named, well, Mr. Beaver, and it concerns the great lion Aslan, who is a Christ figure in the book:

> "Aslan is a lion—*the* Lion, the great Lion."
>
> "Ooh!" said Susan. "I'd thought he was a man. Is he—quite safe? I shall feel rather nervous about meeting a lion." . . .
>
> "Safe?" said Mr Beaver; ". . . Who said anything about safe? 'Course he isn't safe. But he's good. He's the King, I tell you."[2]

Our personal experience isn't broad enough and we're just not wise enough to understand all the whys of God's actions. That's why we need to be careful about basing our theology of God's goodness on our personal circumstances.

WHERE DO YOU GET YOUR THEOLOGY?

As I said before, everyone has a theology of some sort. We are all students in a sense—learning, listening, watching, trying to figure out how life works. But if we're not intentional about deriving our beliefs about God from Scripture, then culture and life experience will form it for us, and these are never dependable sources.

Culture's opinion is temporary, with shifting and changing borders. What is considered true in one decade may be considered demonstrably false in the next—and in both decades it will probably be determined by talking heads who have never had a real experience with God.

And then, as we've seen, there's life experience, which definitely shapes our thinking about God but is likely to lead to flawed, inaccurate conclusions because much of our own life experience derives from the brokenness of our sinful world, not from God's true nature.

We can't form accurate theories of God, for example, from the pain a wounded person caused us. A friend of mine was killed by a drunk driver. God didn't influence that man to drive drunk; he made that decision of his own free will.

Satan, too, is a source for our painful experience in the world, and he often gets off scot-free for the destruction he wreaks in people's lives. How many of us have blamed God for something He didn't cause and made faulty conclusions about His goodness on the basis of that experience? Our pain gets attributed to God when He is actually the one who offers restoration and healing for the pain.

Culture and experience aren't dependable enough to form a sound theology of God's goodness. They're too limited by time and personal perspective. What we don't understand today we may understand tomorrow, or we may not understand until heaven. Which is why it's all the more important to base our theology on something that lasts. Something concrete. Something eternal that can withstand floods, fire, storms, and the test of time. And that is Scripture.

Pain tells us many things, but usually we won't hear it say that God is good. Because the natural response to pain is to search for someone to blame. And as we look for a worthy candidate to hold responsible, Satan's finger is already pointing toward heaven like a blinking neon light.

But in all of this, God is not silent. He stands up for His character, for His goodness, in the middle of every storm. The job of the Holy Spirit in us is to reassure us of what is right, to help us interpret the witness of Scripture and to shape our theology accurately. And He speaks to us always in the context of relationship. As Carolyn Custis James explained:

> The word often used for theology in the Bible is the relational word *know.* Moses used it to express his longing for an intimate relationship with God when he prayed, "If you are pleased with me, teach me your ways so I may *know* you and continue to find favor with you" (Ex. 33:13, emphasis added). David described the benefits of such a relationship when he sang, "Those who know your name [or your character] will trust in you" (Ps. 9:10a, emphasis added). The Hebrew word used in each case is the same word used elsewhere to describe the tender intimate relationship between a husband and wife. For example, Adam was said to *know* his wife Eve, implying both knowledge and intimacy.[3]

In a sense, the depth of our theology of God is related to the depth of our relationship with Him and learning to recognize His still small voice. It's not still and small because it is inferior, but because truth has no need to shout. And the truth He whispers day and night builds on His promise that, if we remain close to Him, His goodness will follow us our whole lives long (Ps. 23:6).

CONVERSATIONS WITH GOD

The Spirit waits to speak to us until He is wanted. When our minds are quieted and our hearts are open, He gently speaks the truth that has the power to free us. One word, one conversation, one experience with God can heal us, clarify our confusion, and inspire us to trust in His goodness again.

One night just several weeks after Haven's death, I lay soaking in my bathtub, where some of my clearest God encounters have happened as well as some of my best creativity. Probably because I'm free from distractions. My kids get locked out and my cell phone put away. It's just me, God, and my thoughts.

I sat talking with God about His decision not to heal Haven. I was struggling to formulate what I now believed about healing and His promises in Scripture. *God, I'm choosing to trust Your ways, but I wish I could understand them. Your Word says that You heal, but in Haven's case You didn't, and I'm so confused by that.*

I wasn't angry, bitter, or resentful. God and I were in a good place, working through my disappointment together. But the prior ten months, particularly the last three, had been brutal to my psyche, so God and I had a lot of emotional trauma to discuss. Not only had He allowed her to die; He had allowed her to go through intense suffering, and she was just a baby. Why would a good God do that?

The pain in my heart had its own narrative that wrestled against biblical truth. My beliefs about God were being tested. Would they hold up under the fire? And what would I believe about Him going forward?

God is not put off by the tension between our narratives and His own. He knew exactly what He was getting Himself into when He chose us. He knew every weakness, every tendency, every choice we'd make. And by some crazy act of grace—because He's good!—He picked us before we had any chance of proving ourselves to Him. God looks past our exterior and our mistakes and sees straight into the hearts of the people He's called us to be. He's committed to making us into those people because He loves us too much to leave us the way He found us. And again, that's because He's incredibly good.

Graciously God has chosen you and me to play a significant part in His grand plan for humanity. You are no understudy in God's plan.

You are a leading character. An incredible, unthinkable, unmatchable inheritance awaits each of us as His children.

This inheritance is not only something we will receive in heaven but also includes a victorious life here on earth. Mind-blowing isn't it? While both heaven and earthly victory have been provided by Jesus, we do have to fight on earth to overcome our daily battles. Which is why we mustn't throw down our end of the rope and walk away from God. It's also why we mustn't pretend with Him. If we never resolve our questions about His goodness, we won't trust Him. If we won't trust Him, we won't follow Him, especially into the dark places where He sometimes goes. And if we won't go to the dark places, we may miss out on our inheritance.

> **YOU ARE NO UNDERSTUDY IN GOD'S PLAN. YOU ARE A LEADING CHARACTER.**

Right now God faithfully holds His side of the rope. He wants us to do our part and engage with Him. He wants us to tug all we want, all we need. But because of His grace, He won't let us win. No matter how much we pull away, He'll tug us back to Him, wooing us with love and healing. He's not likely to explain Himself. But He will grant us a fresh perspective and help us move forward.

HIGHER

That is exactly what happened to me that night in the bathtub. I told God I wanted to understand Him better. I said I was willing to both be honest and hear correction. And as quickly as the words left my mouth that night, He answered—not audibly, but as an impression on my heart. I remember it so clearly: *Stacy, My ways are higher than your ways. My thoughts are higher than your thoughts.*

I felt as if He had turned on a light bulb in my mind. The words were from Isaiah 55:9, which I had read many times in the past, but now they held a different weight for me. They were a fresh word, in season, aimed straight to my heart.

I didn't sense God wagging a holy finger at me while staring arrogantly down His righteous nose, all frustrated that I wasn't catching on sooner. And He wasn't shaming me. He was answering my questions by reminding me that when I can't understand Him, I need to elevate my thinking. While His plans may not always make sense to my finite mind, He operates on a completely different plane than I do. And because His thoughts and plans are high above mine, He has the advantage of knowing what is to come.

In Genesis 15:5, before God gave Abraham a promise for his future, He told him to look up. He wanted Abraham's focus off the trappings of this world and cast heavenward so He could expand Abraham's thinking and rekindle his dreaming. To be able to accept

WHEN I CAN'T UNDERSTAND HIM, I NEED TO ELEVATE MY THINKING.

God's plans for our lives we have to elevate our gaze where the sky is the limit. It's easy to become bogged down by life's disappointments, both great and small, but God's ways and purposes for our lives always include things we can't do through our own strength. We'll never believe His plans are possible if we're staring too long at our unmet expectations and what we can't understand. With such limited perspective, our feet will remain in Harran, and if we stay too long, our dreams may end up dying there.

Jesus has already prepared, charted, and secured our future. He knows intricately the plans He has for us. And each one is good. So in a sense, when He whispers them to our hearts, it is in past tense, coming from a place of already having been secured. Receiving His Word that night continued my healing. Essentially, coaxing me out of Harran.

My need wasn't to find out why He hadn't healed Haven on earth as much as it was to be assured that there *was* a good reason. *My thoughts and ways are higher* confirmed that, yes, there was a purpose greater than I could understand, and because Jesus has already secured it, I will eventually see it. That was enough for me. After that, anytime I'd feel unsettled, I'd go back to that answer.

Our experiences in life, especially the painful ones, can seem to contradict what we thought we knew of God. Perhaps He allowed our dreams of a happy, lasting marriage to die. We prayed over the relationship, we went to counseling, we compromised, we begged, and after all that our spouse still left. Though we know God didn't cause the divorce, He didn't prevent it, and beneath layers of confusion, we begin to think that makes Him culpable. We know we should go to God for strength, but wasn't it His hand that could have prevented the breakup in the first place? Maybe it's not as easy to trust Him as it once was. In fact, we may start to question things we once believed. Like Haven's chemotherapy, our faith didn't "work," and we wonder if it ever will.

In times like that, doubt may cling to us like a dryer sheet. Just when we think we've placed it out of sight and out of mind, someone taps us on the shoulder and says, "Excuse me, but you've got something stuck on your backside."

I WANT ANSWERS

God is with you in the storm. While it's 100 percent true, it doesn't completely explain why a good God would allow the storm in the first place. I'd very much prefer for God to prevent the pain altogether. But the Bible is full of stories of those who experienced heartache in the midst of a good God. Women were raped. Job lost everything. Children were sold or born into slavery. Women were treated as second-class citizens or worse. People were beaten or killed. Life could be brutal in biblical times, and we see that in the pages of Scripture.

But the fact that something is in the Bible doesn't mean that God wanted it that way. Remember, the Bible is not only the Word of God; it's also a record of ancient history. The people in it experienced real life, including real pain. Many of those who were hurt were left with no solid answer as to why. And not all of their stories ended in justice, which of course is unsettling. Many of the raped women were either killed (Num. 31:15) or forced to marry their rapists (Deut. 21:10–14). Though Job was given more children, he never got back the ones he lost—and this was a man who "feared God and shunned evil" (Job 1:1). How do we reason with that?

It's hard to reconcile pain when we have trusted God to prevent it. And isn't trust the crux of our relationship with Him? A good God who allows pain seems like a math equation you expect to solve neatly but end up with a remainder you don't know what to do with. God is good + I serve Him = a good life for me. It's far too simplistic, but deep down that's what we expect. If we didn't expect it, we'd never be disappointed when something traumatic happens—like a daughter being diagnosed with a brain tumor and dying in her mother's arms.

Yes, there is definitely a floating remainder in my theology, and I have no idea where to put it. I think it's fair to want an answer. Don't you?

THE SEED OF SCARCITY

Reconciling the pain in our lives with the claim that God is always good means answering the idea that He might have withheld good from us. This was the same slant Satan used with Eve in the garden.

All he had to do was plant the seed of scarcity in her mind, the idea that maybe, just maybe, God was keeping something good from her. Once that idea was planted, the next thought was predictable: *If He's withholding it, that means I'm lacking it.* It's a subtle accusation, but it's an incredibly effective way of undermining trust.

In Eve's case, the good that Satan said God was withholding was knowledge packed inside the fruit that hung from the branch Satan's cold body was twisted on. He lied about that fruit, telling Eve it was forbidden because it possessed the power to make her like God. And Eve fell for the lie. Generations later, with God's words recorded on paper, we can turn a couple of pages to the right in our Bibles and read the devastating consequences of her choice. But her only option at the time was to operate from the trust she had built in God's good character. And the seed of scarcity was directly undermining that trust.

Possibly the saddest part of this entire event was that Eve chose to lean into lack instead of leaning into God's abundance. At her fingertips was an overflowing surplus of everything she would ever need. She and Adam had the pleasure of perfect weather, great sex, farm-to-table organic food, strong bodies without the unwanted muffin top (I can dream, right?), and daily communion with God. What more could she possibly ask for? And why didn't she see that she was *already* like God, formed in His image?

Because Eve's finite mind couldn't comprehend God's motive for forbidding the fruit, she did what seemed right to her and tasted it. When she swallowed the seed of scarcity, it grew into mistrust. While the juice was still dripping down her chin, bitter regret birthed shame, and the rest is unfortunate history.

I'm not so far removed from Eve. The same humanity operating in her lives in me. The same enemy who convinced her to doubt God's goodness too often convinces me. I'm prone to swallow the seed of scarcity when I work hard yet see other people being promoted. Or when my friend's pictures on Facebook look polished and perfect, with their flawless hair and white teeth, compared to my tarnished and imperfect life. Or when everyone else is getting prayers answered and dreams fulfilled, and I'm still waiting on God. When I'm not getting what I think I need, it's so easy to assume that God is holding out on me. When I can't understand God's motives, perhaps I taste the fruit too. Then the mistrust starts growing.

Can you relate? Maybe you've said the same prayer for a husband the last fifteen years, but it's beginning to look as if every good single man is taken. The only men you can find have no jobs, hate life, and still live with their mommas. You and your aging ovaries are beginning to suspect that God enjoys watching you struggle or simply doesn't want your dreams to materialize. It feels like rejection, like being on the wrong end of favoritism. When life runs smoothly, you're able to sweep your struggle under the rug, but when circumstances trigger your deferred desires, scarcity thinking emerges again. Disappointment, depression, anxiety, and anger rush in like a flood.

THE CONSUMER FALLACY?

Perhaps one reason behind this tendency is that deep down we hold a subtle belief that it is God's job to make life easier for us. If I had to give a name to this attitude, it would be *entitlement*. We feel entitled to something from God, especially if we believe we've done what God wants. If we put a quarter's worth of prayer into the heavenly vending machine, we should be able to turn the dial and get a blessing out. A quarter's worth of reading my Bible, and out pops the best parking space. A quarter's worth of tithing, and I receive a handful of money. If God is good, shouldn't He do His part when I do mine?

I wish I didn't have a tendency to think this way, but I do. This is our consumer mindset at work: *I'm paying God with my service, and as the customer, I should get what I want in return.* Part of us believes, maybe unconsciously, that we own a share in the company, that we have power over His decisions. The problem is our narrow worldview and a Bible interpretation that is filtered through our desire for comfort and control.

I can't find anywhere in Scripture, from the book of Genesis to Revelation, where God says we'll have a painless life or even an immediate answer to our requests. God doesn't promise easy. Every person ever mentioned in the Bible lived a life laced with tragedy as well as triumph—even Jesus. He suffered greatly during His last three years on this earth, and His last days were agony. Yet we never hear one word from His mouth accusing God of wrong. God doesn't promise easy. Instead of easy, Jesus said to take up our cross and follow Him. His footsteps went straight to Calvary.

In the Garden of Gethsemane, Jesus' theology of His Father collided with His life experience. The way He handled it can teach us how to navigate disappointment. First, He begged God to change His mind about the cross. His flesh didn't want to suffer and die, and He was honest about that. His struggle was so intense that blood vessels burst beneath His skin. But as blood escaped His body, so did His will. When God's decision went unchanged, Jesus came to terms with

GOD DOESN'T PROMISE EASY.

God's will being better than His. He bowed His knee to His Father and said, "Not my will, but yours be done" (Luke 22:42). And it was settled.

Jesus made the choice for His body to be crucified only because His will was put to death first. When He walked out of Gethsemane, He was already a crucified man. And I don't believe any of this would have been possible if He hadn't been completely convinced that His Father is good and all His ways are perfect.

That's true for us too. We won't be able to settle our disappointment if we don't crucify our wills in the Garden with Jesus and place our trust in the goodness of our Father.

I believe that God heals, wants us to be prosperous, and gives us not just our needs but also the desire of our hearts. But the longer I'm alive, the more I realize that I live to serve at the pleasure of God. When I look back to the saints of old in Scripture, I see how they, like Jesus, became offerings poured out for God. Instead of focusing on their needs, wants, or rights, they focused on who they were serving.

WHO IS YOUR LORD?

Have you ever wondered what the fundamental question of the Bible is? No? To be honest, me neither. But I recently learned that the question above all questions is this: who is your Lord? It's the subject of the same struggle that took place in two different gardens, Eden and Gethsemane, but with very different outcomes. Eve fell subject to her will; Jesus conquered His.

The question is: who is our Lord?

The answer: whatever we refuse to nail to the cross. If it escapes the nails and it's not God, then it's an idol.

The cities along Abraham's journey from Ur to Canaan by way of Harran were littered with idols. Some cities served multiple gods. At every turn there must have been hills holding carved stones or wooden images lifted high for people to bow down before. I wonder if Abraham sometimes fought the urge to revert to his idol-worshiping days and offer sacrifices to some handmade image he felt he could better understand than this unseen God who was leading him down an unknown road to a still-uncertain future.

What are our idols? They could be our expectations. Our perceived rights. Our disappoint-

WHO IS YOUR LORD? IT'S THE SUBJECT OF THE SAME STRUGGLE THAT TOOK PLACE IN TWO DIFFERENT GARDENS, EDEN AND GETHSEMANE.

ment or our need to understand God's will. Every idol is a hollow substitution for God's better way. If we're not willing to smash them or crucify them, that's a good sign that they have become gods to us.

It's interesting to me that though Jesus understood why the cross was necessary, He still struggled to accept it. We want to know why. We demand to know why. But if we're told why, that doesn't mean we'd accept it, because wanting our own way seems to be hardwired into our human flesh. No wonder we have such a tendency to insist on our own way when bowing our knee to the Father is the only way forward.

Can pain be an idol in our lives? Disappointment? I think so. Though no one consciously wants it around, I think we may sometimes, inadvertently, build a shrine for it. We've become one with our hurts and unmet expectations, and following Jesus forward would mean getting rid of what is familiar, even strangely comforting. But to experience the great inheritance that awaits us, we must move out of the desolate land of idols and keep our eyes on the goodness of Jesus.

I'M OFFENDED

When life doesn't go our way, we can easily find ourselves in a volatile place of frustration with God where we are most tempted to get offended by Him. We currently live in a national culture of offense. As my friend Robert Madu has observed, "It seems like everybody, everywhere is perpetually offended about everything all the time. . . . And being easily offended is no longer seen as a weakness in your character, but is now your constitutional right."[4]

Men, women, married people, single people, Christians, atheists, Baptists, Catholics, Pentecostals, you name it, have taken offense at something and are wearing it like a badge of honor. Subconsciously, maybe we feel responsible to meet a daily quota of offense and tally it with a notch on our belts. If we haven't met the quota, then we get on social media to find something to be offended over. We look for statements opposing our political views or the way we raise our kids, and we give the offending "friend" a piece of our minds in forty characters or less.

I recently read that a group of people were offended by Chick-fil-A because they don't serve hamburgers. Imagine the audacity of a chicken-based restaurant not serving beef! How insensitive to beef lovers everywhere. That's obviously ridiculous, but it's not really that far-fetched. I've read posts on Facebook bashing churches, neighbors, even the checkout lady at the grocery store because her customer service wasn't as friendly as it should have been.

Honestly, when did we become so entitled? Or maybe we have always been, only now we have a platform to voice it. The sheer volume of people who are offended and the silliness of what we're getting offended over would be comical if it weren't so sad.

I realize there are some serious topics today that stir our desire for justice and need someone to stand up and speak about them, but I'm not referring to those things. I'm simply pointing out that our present culture has made offense trendy and is expecting everyone to get on the bandwagon to bitterness. This is damaging on so many levels, but none more than in our relationship with God. When our expectations aren't met, when God says no to what we're asking for, when He doesn't respond our way right away, when we hurt or even feel the slightest bit of discomfort, do we get offended because He actually has the audacity to be God and do what He thinks is right? How dare He serve us chicken when we asked for a burger! How dare He not treat us, the customer, as always right!

We need to check ourselves regularly to be reminded that God doesn't owe us anything, though in His goodness He gives us so much. Let's not go down this slippery slope and crash and burn into bitterness. Instead, let's be countercultural and fight vehemently against offense, especially in our relationship with Christ. Let's put our own agendas aside and focus on His. Instead of looking for what we can get, let's focus on what we can give. Not our will, but His, be done.

Offense puts skewed lenses over the eyes of our hearts, making it impossible to see God properly. Though nothing has actually changed and God is still flooding you with love, His funnel from heaven looks like it's pouring sand instead of blessing. A lens of offense will convince us that God is indifferent to our pain, that He simply doesn't care. That hurts us. And if He hurts me, we assume, then He's not completely good. And if He's not completely good, then we can't trust Him. We hold God at fault because He chose His good and perfect will instead of what we mistakenly believed we were entitled to.

I'm both convicted and inspired when I hear that Christians in antiquity counted it a privilege to be persecuted. Beaten, imprisoned, stoned, even being sawed in half or fed to lions, they suffered for the name of Christ. While the experience was frightening and undoubtedly painful, they considered it their highest honor. Even today, in countries hostile to Christianity, believers are imprisoned and killed regularly for their faith. Most of us in the Western world can't imagine this kind of mentality; we get flustered when God doesn't give us the parking spot we ask for.

I'm not saying that to be righteous we must be persecuted for the gospel. I am saying that we should learn from those who were willing to bow their wills to God's despite what it cost them. We should lay down our offense and entitlement and pick up our cross.

In this broken world, pain and joy are inescapably intertwined. I'm not sure where the idea came from that we're entitled to a struggle-free life when Jesus told us plainly that struggle is guaranteed for us: "I have told you these things, so that in me you may have peace. In this world you will have trouble. But take heart! I have overcome the world" (John 16:33).

Jesus said that trouble will come, that it's basically inevitable. He also said we will find peace in Him because He has already overcome the pain in the world. So where have we gotten off balance? Where have we gotten the idea that everything is supposed to go our way and that if it doesn't, that's a sign that God isn't good?

Perhaps it's our incessant human longing for pleasure. Or perhaps we've developed a skewed idea of what good is. Good doesn't always mean pleasure. It means that what benefits us brings God glory and builds God's kingdom, where we will ultimately reign together with Him.

When Jesus is Lord over our lives, there is no room for entitlement. There is no battle of wills. We are submitted to what He chooses in His goodness and wisdom.

I hope you choose that for yourself. I hope you fall at His feet in surrender. Let's choose it together right here and now. Forfeiting isn't worth it. Your relationship with God is too vital, too precious, too healing to be broken.

Paul said in Galatians 5:7, "You were running a good race. Who cut in on you to keep you from obeying the truth?" For many of us it's not who, but what. What have we emotionally married? What has made us hit a dead end? Is it entitlement, offense, or disappointment that keeps us from moving forward?

If you base what you believe to be true of God on what happens to you in life, you will wrestle with God to your grave. But if you make the choice to give up your will and move forward in His, God will meet you where you are. And then you will truly "taste and see that the LORD is good" (Ps. 34:8).

TEN

PURPOSE IN PAIN

No matter what level our pain is, God can give it purpose. In fact, its function can be far more glorious than we ever dreamed if we let what the book of Ruth refers to as the threshing floor do its work.

In ancient days, the threshing floor was an essential part of harvest for farmers. Seated on a flat-topped hill, it was the place where grain was crushed to remove the useless chaff—husks, dirt, and the like. The farmer usually used a pair of oxen to walk on top of the stalks of grain, mashing them underfoot. He then scooped up the pulverized material with his winnowing fork and threw it high in the air.

Threshing floors were located on the tops of hills because the wind played a significant role in the process. As the breeze blew, it caught the lighter-weight chaff and carried it away as the heavier, more valuable grain fell at the farmer's feet. With the chaff removed, the grain was now ready for use.

If we choose, our pain can serve as a threshing floor for our souls, where God can do a number of miraculous things. He draws us closer to His heart, where we can see Him more clearly than before. He brings greater glory to His name as the hindrances in our lives are removed. And He matures us by refinement so we become more like Him.

We may not realize this is happening at the time. We just know we are hurting and are trying to make it through each day. For a while we may feel nothing but the crushing. But that is just the start of a purposeful transformation in us. On this high, breezy hill, lesser concerns will be winnowed and will fall away. We will seek God more desperately and find Him in deeper places than ever before— not because God enjoys hiding from us or watching us suffer, but because pain tends to bend our knees, putting us in a posture to seek Him in a way no other experience can. We'll seek Him more because we need Him more. And out of this greater need we'll read the Bible differently, pray differently, and thirst for His voice differently. Sleep will be less important than the urgency to be with Jesus. Formality will go by the wayside. And our level of hunger to be with Jesus will be matched by our revelation of Him.

> PAIN TENDS TO BEND OUR KNEES, PUTTING US IN A POSTURE TO SEEK HIM IN A WAY NO OTHER EXPERIENCE CAN.

GOD ENCOUNTERS

A few years ago a three-year-old boy in our church contracted an infection that put him near death in the ICU for weeks. One day when I came to visit, his mom and I had a God encounter that shifted her outlook not only of God but of her struggle with fear and doubt.

Cari explained to me that she had been seized with paralyzing fear during the nights she stayed with Talby, her son. Watching him struggle for life with monitors and tubes connected all over his body triggered her most painful emotions. She had begun dreading the night hours and desperately needed God to help her. Sitting there in the waiting room, she and I asked the Lord to reveal Himself in her situation.

As we quietly waited on God to speak truth to Cari's heart, she broke the silence. "I see a picture of Jesus standing over Talby's bed with His arms extended in protection. His enormous presence is filling the dark room with light." That revelation may seem simple, but it was a defining moment for Cari. From then on she no longer feared the nights because she chose to believe God's revelation of truth, and it set her free. Cari had always known that God was with Talby, but only when she was in a situation of desperate need did she see God in such a clear and powerful way.

That kind of God encounter is often a part of being on the threshing floor. And such encounters change us because what we know in our heads about God becomes experiential.

When I speak of God encounters, I'm not referring to the constant presence of the Holy Spirit, who is with us at all times. I'm talking about those times when Jesus reveals Himself to us in our situation or we receive a revelation in His presence that shifts something inside us. I remember several of these in my life—specific times when I connected powerfully with the Lord while in prayer or worship or when reading my Bible.

One in particular came during a time of worship at a women's conference. I had been dealing with a wound of a friend's betrayal. Even though she had wronged me initially, I felt it was my fault we were at an impasse in our relationship. I was carrying a sense of condemnation and felt as if God was disappointed in me for being hurt by what the other person had done.

In the middle of worship that day, I felt the Holy Spirit's presence. In the gentlest, most tender way, I felt Him say, *I'm sorry she hurt you.*

And the weight of my guilt lifted because I realized I didn't have to feel guilty for being hurt. From then on I saw the situation differently, which made it easier to forgive.

We don't have to be at a women's conference to have God encounters, of course. We can be driving in the car, praying at home, cooking dinner, standing in church—whatever. God encounters can happen wherever the Lord shows up and speaks to our hearts.

In the year we fought for Haven's life, my need for God was like kindling, sparking a fire of longing to know Him more. My prayer was always to see God's hand heal my daughter. But as time went on, and especially after her death, my prayer shifted. Now I wanted more than anything to see His face so I could know Him better. I yearned to get a better sense of what He was like, even if I didn't understand what I was seeing. Reading the Word, intentionally allowing God into my grief, sitting with the Holy Spirit, worshiping, and regularly staying connected to church even when I'd rather stay home and soak in my tears reminded me that there's more about Him that I don't know, but that I could trust what I knew thus far.

I can honestly say that I knew God better and more richly during my time of greatest pain than I knew Him before it. Where else but on the threshing floor would I be so desperate for this kind of knowing?

Even better, it was through this desperation, this seeking and finding, that I matured. This is part of pain's purpose in our lives.

THE CASE FOR MATURITY

Both the world and the body of Christ are in critical need of mature believers. The harvest of hearts is ready for reaping, but the workers in His kingdom are relatively few. We've grown comfortable, lost our sharpness, and settled into lackadaisical patterns. And as far as I can tell, this is not strictly a twenty-first-century issue, but the way of our flesh since the beginning of time.

The writer of Hebrews admonished a group of New Testament believers for still relying on milk for spiritual nourishment when they should have been off the bottle by now.

> Though by this time you ought to be teachers, you need someone
> to teach you the elementary truths of God's word all over again.
> You need milk, not solid food! Anyone who lives on milk, being still
> an infant, is not acquainted with the teaching about righteousness.
> But solid food is for the mature, who by constant use have trained
> themselves to distinguish good from evil.
>
> (Heb. 5:12–14)

Even those ancient saints resisted moving toward maturity because the process wasn't easy. Instead of following the voice of the Holy Spirit in their personal lives, they still let their flesh govern their actions. But if we look just four verses before, the writer had contrasted their behavior to that of Christ's and told us one of the processes of maturity: "Son though he was, he learned obedience from what he suffered" (Heb. 5:8). Clearly, these believers had *not* learned obedience. The path of least resistance seemed right to them. They were looking for life's easy button. Good enough had become good enough.

But good enough is not enough for God. And it should never be good enough for us when it comes to spiritual maturity. He is looking for mature men and women to bring in the people who are ready to receive Christ. And He is willing to use our suffering to teach us and help us grow.

The thing about the grain on the threshing floor is that it has no control over the process. It can't stop the giant ox from pulverizing it or make the wind quit blowing it. It is more or less powerless, just as you and I are in difficult times. We usually can't make our situation change or go away. But there is one thing we have control of, and that is the response of our hearts. We can harden or yield them to the Lord. But we will not mature unless we yield ourselves to the Holy Spirit and come to the threshing floor.

There are times when God allows us to throw our fits, but as we mature, our fits become less and less frequent. The process of sanctification that the Holy Spirit works in our souls has the purpose of making us more like Christ. It's not magical. It's not instant. There's no easy button. And it hurts—oh, how it can hurt. But it is through yielding to the Holy Spirit that our souls undergo a spiritual metamorphosis. Over time our thoughts, our desires, our ways will change. We will be pressed, then winnowed. And God allows this, not to destroy us, but so that our hindrances, our idols, and our wills that compete with His are defeated.

What does this process feel like? The apostle Paul described it vividly:

> Though we experience every kind of pressure, we're not crushed.
> At times we don't know what to do, but quitting is not an option.
> We are persecuted by others, but God has not forsaken us. We may
> be knocked down, but not out. We continually share in the death
> of Jesus in our own bodies so that the resurrection life of Jesus will
> be revealed through our humanity.
>
> (2 Cor. 4:8–10 TPT)

Through the entire process we are never alone. The Farmer is there every moment. Carefully He lifts us in His winnowing fork and gives us over to the wind of the Spirit, which gently carries the chaff away. What is left in us is weightier, more useful, and falls at our Master's feet.

But our maturing process isn't over at that point, though I would love for it to be. The threshing floor isn't a onetime experience in which we are made perfect once and for all. It's a lifetime process of surrender and change as we try to reflect Christ better.

Because we'll be on the threshing floor a lot over the course of a lifetime, it's important we realize that it's not a punishment. There are times when we'll go there intentionally as we follow in Jesus' steps and suffer accordingly. Even if our struggle is a consequence of our own disobedience, God can still use it as a tool to grow us. We must know that during the process, it is our wills, our flesh, that will be crushed, not our souls. God carefully protects us within His hands.

While it's not a comfortable place, the threshing floor is a divine place. This is counterintuitive to what we're often taught about God, isn't it? And it can be confusing on many different levels.

The Holy Spirit is supposed to lead us to victory, after all. Which may lead us to wonder, *Doesn't victory feel better than this?*

LESSONS FROM DISCOMFORT

My brother is in the military, and I've learned from him that nothing is comfortable about being a soldier. He's spent many a night lying on the freezing cold ground in a sleeping bag, eating—or should I say choking down?—MREs and living in other countries far away from family for a year or more at a time. But I've seen such growth in him from what he's experienced. He's better at disciplining his body and heeding authority and has learned that he can endure far more than he thought he could. He's become more of a man.

Who ever said that growth is easy? But it is so worth it!

Somehow I tend to expect the divine to be nothing but beautiful, but sometimes it arrives in unexpected, even unattractive forms. Jesus arrived on earth as a red, wrinkled, crying infant instead of a conquering King. I imagine that many people who encountered Him as an adult rejected Him because the Divine Answer didn't look like their idea of a Messiah. They'd expected the long-awaited Savior to be famed and heroic—which Jesus was, of course, but He was also humble, merciful, and gracious. So as the Divine stood right before their eyes, they turned away looking for something more suitable.

I believe our transformations on the threshing floor can look unexpected too. We may say words like "Jesus, make me more like You," but do we really expect to be stomped on, picked up with a fork, blown by the wind, and dropped on the floor? When that happens, we may well find ourselves rebuking the pain God has allowed—or even God Himself.

Instead of doing that, let us appreciate, dare I even say celebrate, the role of the threshing floor in transforming our lives. Its purpose is not to harm us, only to remove what is hindering us.

In this place, Jesus is the Master, the Boss. Pain works for Him, and He works it to our advantage so that it becomes a tool to bring about His functional purposes in our lives. Sifted through His hands, what was meant to destroy us builds us up instead.

Maybe you're in a hard season and can relate to what an ox treading on your flesh feels like. You labor to breathe, and if you could, you would throw that giant animal off you. But God is asking you to trust Him. Trust that He won't leave you there alone. Trust that the purposes He can create from your pain will be far better than you can imagine. Trust that your time on the threshing floor is transforming you to reflect the glory of God.

THE FREEDOM ROAD

The road of spiritual maturation leads to something else we all need: freedom. But travel on that road isn't always easy. Faulty thought processes, habitual responses, and unwise choices can slow us down, and unhelpful attitudes such as fear, bitterness, or insecurity can tie weights to our feet. Pain has a way of exposing these hindrances.

If you want to know where you struggle in life, observe your response when pressure is applied—such as when someone cuts you off in traffic. Just the other day a truck pulled out in front of me so fast that its wheels squealed on the asphalt; then it proceeded to drive along at thirty-five miles an hour. Judging by the words that went through my head (and possibly came out of my mouth) when I slammed on my brakes, I still need more sanctification in the area of grace and patience.

Trials help us wrestle with our hearts' hindrances by showing what is pulling us down and holding us back. To lighten our load, we are to listen and yield to the voice of the Holy Spirit that comes either through His written Word or through the impressions He speaks to our hearts. What the Holy Spirit said to me that day, after I had called the driver a few choice names, had something to do with controlling my attitude and speaking words of life and encouragement.

Now, a case of minor road rage seems simple to change compared to the disappointment and doubt that result from losing a child, but the process is the same—hearing and heeding the voice of the Spirit. Each time we do that, our hindrances become lighter and we mature in faith. But like the church in Hebrews, we will stay stuck if we hear but don't heed.

God's Word is like a mirror that reflects the true nature of our hearts. Pity the woman who sees herself in that mirror but resists what the Word says.

Recently I was talking with a woman who was clearly living outside the boundaries of God's Word and it was wounding her. She wanted help, but she also desperately wanted to keep living the way she was and for God to be okay with it. In our conversation I tried to lovingly shed light on Scripture, not to condemn her but to help free her. "We're all broken people. Every one of us. But when we submit to God's Word, He does a work of healing within," I told her. I wanted so badly to see her chains broken. But I could see in her eyes that she didn't want to look into the mirror of God's Word, which would confront her—but could also heal her. I knew then that she would sadly remain bound. She walked away from our conversation the same woman as when we started, maybe even a little more bitter.

> **THE CALLING ON MY LIFE REQUIRES A WOMAN, NOT A CHILD. THAT'S TRUE FOR YOUR LIFE TOO.**

God works from the inside out. His purposes aren't always to free us from our situation, but to free us from our restraints. He'll use our circumstances to do it because He wastes nothing—neither pain nor struggle, not even our bad decisions. Everything in His hands can be used for His master plan and purposes.

The outward change we're looking for may not happen until we have found inner freedom. And that is part of pain's purpose—to break us loose from what is tying us up inside. Haven's death crushed me, but as I learned to internally push through fear, doubt, and disappointment by the power of the Holy Spirit, I became freer and freer.

The calling on my life requires a woman, not a child. That's true for your life too. I want us all to find freedom so that we can walk the path of maturity.

FOR HIS GLORY

God used Abraham in the mightiest of ways. "Father of Many Nations" is no small title, and it didn't come cheap. Nothing of worth ever does. The testing of Abraham's faith broadened his spiritual shoulders so he could withstand the pressure that came with his calling.

If it turns out that pain is one of God's instruments of choice for maturing us, His way of broadening our shoulders for the future, we must consider whether we're still open to that growth. Will we continue to move forward by clinging to Jesus or get lost in bewilderment, unable to understand why He won't remove our painful circumstances?

The world is desperately in need of believers who will make that choice. People are searching for someone to show them the way to victory, someone who has fought the fight of faith and overcome discouragement and doubt. If we stay the course and let our pain be our crossroads to maturity, people will be changed by watching the change in us.

Have your dreams gone up in flames and left a big, stinking pile of ash? Don't throw it away. God doesn't. Instead, He transforms the ashes into something beautiful. This is God being God, making miracles from our messes to bring glory and honor to His name. And we are invited to be part of that magnificent transformation. But it might not happen just the way we expect.

We all have plans that seem right in our own eyes. It made sense to me that God would get the most glory if He healed Haven. Word would travel like brushfire. There were people all around the world praying for her. Our situation had been mentioned on a national Christian television program and featured on CBS. We worked at a ten-thousand-member church well connected with other churches around the globe.

Can you imagine the stir that Haven's healing would have caused? A child marked for certain death, then miraculously healed from brain cancer. I couldn't imagine why God would choose to end this story any other way but with healing. Why would He risk His reputation? Why not show the world how powerful He is? Why would He not heal your marriage? Why would He not give you the promotion?

Logically, I thought my plan would be the best way to make God's name great. But I've learned that my logic is always inferior to God's. And if I'm truthful with myself, I've come to see that sometimes buried in what I believe are noble plans is really the desire for my will to be done and for what I want to be achieved. I'm trying to make peace with the reality that God alone knows how best to make His name great.

I admit that I prefer it when God chooses to work through outward displays of miracles, signs, and wonders. And I believe God wants us to ask for the things that are in heaven, such as healing, freedom, and blessing, to be done here on earth. So one of the things I'm asking of God this year is to have more demonstration of the Holy Spirit's power in my life. I want to pray for more people and see them healed and have more words of knowledge and encouragement for others. I think God wants us all to operate more in these spiritual gifts, just as Jesus did while He was on earth.

But I also want to not feel condemned and second-rate when God chooses to demonstrate His power through me in other ways. If God doesn't heal when I pray, then I want to be able to say, "I did what I was supposed to do. I opened the door for God to move, and I'm not going to quit praying for people." After all, it's God's decision what He does with what I give Him, and I don't want to discount any of His decisions. Maybe the person I prayed for wasn't ready to receive healing. Maybe God has other plans. Maybe I'll never know. (I write this in a meager effort to bring balance to my own heart, because when

God doesn't do what I ask, I tend to either feel shame or give up and quit asking.)

I do think it's important to keep in mind that while we're asking for outward displays of miracles, signs, and wonders, God is also performing inward miracles in our souls. Do we consider those second rate? I think they need to be equally appreciated and sought after. What if sustaining a person through hell on earth is the greater miracle than a dramatic healing? What if God's joy breathing strength into a heart transforms a life? What if the wonder is my testimony of God's goodness when I've been through gut-wrenching pain?

That's not to say we should stop believing in outward miracles; God does still perform those today. He still heals bodies, conquers cancer, and even raises the dead. Just recently I prayed for a woman who had ringing in her ears, and after the prayer the ringing was gone. God's power hasn't weakened, and His desire to heal hasn't diminished.

But we mustn't discount the internal miracles, which are as much a sign of His power as someone rising from their grave. When Jesus healed the paralyzed man in Matthew 9, He also healed his spirit by forgiving him of sin. We are triune beings with a body, a soul, and a spirit. The totality of who we are needs healing and changing because every part of us needs freedom from brokenness.

After All That

People have told me time and again that they admire my strength and resilience. They usually follow up by saying they can't imagine getting through the loss of a child. And though there is always a temptation to remind them that I had no choice, I do understand what they mean. I did make a choice to continue following Jesus through my pain.

But make no mistake; it was His power working in my choice that sustained me through heartbreak.

Resilience is a miracle of God, far bigger and more important than we usually think. And this miracle is within the reach of all of us. My family's ten-month battle consisted of a tumor diagnosis, a sudden move to another city, two brain surgeries, ten weeks of chemotherapy, a dank hotel, the birth and care of a new baby, the miracle of an apartment, ten days in isolation, a mind-numbing treatment routine, a ten-week evaluation, a terminal diagnosis, tornadoes, a sudden move back home, an ambulance ride and hospital stays, and the death of my firstborn, the sacred reward of my womb, in my arms. And after all that—*all that*—I am still standing. Do you think that has much to do with me?

I'm here to tell you it has everything to do with the grace of God. As I said, I made the decision to run to Jesus and follow His lead. But then again, it was He who enabled me to do that in the first place.

After all you've been through—bankruptcy, depression, divorce, anxiety, abuse, infertility (insert whatever you're dealing with)—you are still standing too. Maybe you're leaning a bit, but you're still alive. So through *all* that, I say: may God be glorified.

Why do I say that? Because I know me. I know my tendencies to be discouraged and place blame, my tendencies to want answers and immediate justice. To still love Jesus after such disappointment is none other than the work of the Holy Spirit. To still believe and trust Him through my doubt is the grace of God. And I believe it is for you too. He alone deserves all the praise.

Living to tell our story of the work of God in our lives is nothing short of a miracle. But that miracle is not just to make us feel better. God doesn't just have purpose for allowing our pain; He wants us to make purpose *from* our pain.

You Have Something to Say

Every face at the long, rectangular conference table turned toward me. "Why is everyone looking at me?" I asked. "There is no way I'm doing this," I added. "Absolutely not. Never."

Casey had just announced that Keypoint Church would be adding another Sunday morning service to one of our church's locations. He'd pointed out that this addition would leave a vacancy for a speaker to fill while he preached at another campus. And then he'd turned to me. "I believe you're the one who is supposed to preach this service," he said in front of everyone sitting there.

Way to put me on the spot! What was he thinking? Casey knew I struggled with intense stage fright and that I didn't feel equipped to prepare and practice a weekly message. Not to mention that I had three kids at home and barely enough time to keep them fed and my house in order. You could write your name in the dust on my furniture, and he wanted me to preach every single weekend? I appreciated his vote of confidence, but he definitely overestimated my capacity.

"Look, I'm okay with preaching Mother's Day once a year, but every week is too much to ask." Unfortunately, neither Casey nor God agreed. As frantically as I reached for excuses, neither of them would let it go. The challenge for me to step up was like a nagging mosquito that I'd swat away, but that kept coming back.

"Why me, God?" I whined. "Why must I do this?"

Because you have something to say.

Since saying yes to that call several years ago, I have preached nearly every weekend that I'm in town because God really has given me something to say. I've studied the Bible, taken courses, educated myself on public speaking, read book after book, but my words still aren't perfect and my delivery is still flawed. Plus, I still get nervous, and when I get nervous, my Southern drawl comes out. But I keep doing it because I've determined that God didn't bring me through what I've endured for me to remain silent.

You have something to say, too, and you don't need a public platform to say it. There are listening ears all around you—your neighbor, those you work with, the woman in your yoga class, people who want to hear your story. They are looking for someone to tell them that their suffering has meaning and that they can walk through it in victory. And you can be that someone. You don't need to be schooled in public speaking or biblical hermeneutics. You only need your story and a listening ear.

Revelation 12:11 says we overcome the enemy "by the blood of the Lamb and by the word of [our] testimony."

Our victory was made possible by the blood of Jesus, which made a way for our triumph over Satan's attacks. So that part is done for us. Our part is to testify of God's greatness in our lives.

Most of us underestimate what a powerful tool for good our mouths can be. Yet the Holy Spirit tells us it is also one of our God-given weapons to subdue our enemy. Testifying about the goodness of God plants seeds of the gospel in other people's hearts. They are inspired when they hear of our resilience, encouraged when they learn of our struggles. And because actions often speak louder than words, when they see us look to God, they want to look to Him too. I know I do when I see others who have struggled but have pressed on. I'm encouraged when they tell of their battles and scars, their wins and, yes, even their losses, because it reminds me that mine won't destroy me.

Don't underestimate what your testimony does in your own heart as well. Hearing yourself speak of God's goodness reinforces truth in your soul. Consider many of David's psalms. And yet our mouths can easily be rendered silent if they are too busy chewing on doubt and disappointment, which the enemy would love to use to silence us. God may allow the struggle, but for an entirely different reason: to build us.

Struggling doesn't always mean we're weak, so we shouldn't over-analyze it. We struggle because we each have a voice, and by no means does Satan want us to use it for good.

So testify. Tell of God's great love and mercy, of how He brought you through and the threshing floor made you stronger, wiser, more like Christ.

When I battled stage fright, before I stepped foot on a platform, I always recited to myself: "I'm preaching today to give God glory, and every word out of my mouth is going to make the enemy pay for what he's done." So many times, these words gave me the motivating fuel to push through my fear. Now I actually look forward to Sundays when I'm able to speak of what God has done.

How to Maintain a Healthy Heart

Whatever the pain in our lives, we can be pain's master if we use it the right way. But we can only go as far as our hearts are healthy.

I'm not talking about the muscle-pump in our chests. I'm talking about the center of our souls. And one of the best ways I know to keep my heart healthy is to become adept at emptying out negative emotions, such as disappointment and doubt.

I'm a purger. I love the feeling of throwing things away, especially old shoes and clothes. The more I get rid of, the cleaner and more organized my closet is able to be. But it's taken me a little more time to purge my negative emotions. I'm learning it's a good idea to take a regular inventory of our disappointment and doubt. If we find it stored up, then let's empty it. We can get rid of what is holding us down by acknowledging that we were hurt by what happened or didn't happen to us. If we admit it to ourselves and to God, then release it to Him and ask for the right perspective, we'll almost certainly feel lighter.

I've found that the discipline of journaling is a helpful and cathartic tool for this process of purging. I started doing this during our first week in the hospital with Haven because I needed a way to process the thoughts and questions that were racing through my mind. If I had allowed the negative emotions to pile up without recognizing them, I think I would have become hopelessly entangled in them. As I read back through those early journals, I see that giving words to my pain definitely helped me process it and release it.

A healthy heart isn't accomplished haphazardly. It is intentional, sought after, and fought for. And mourning our losses is an important heart-healthy practice. It's okay to miss what we once had—a dream, a relationship, a desire, whatever you cherished that was ripped from your hands. And it's healthy to give those bare hands permission to ache.

Grief is uncomfortable, and the urge to run away from it is normal. But part of healing is taking time to sift through the disappointment, anger, brokenness, and cynicism that may be part of our grief, then consciously releasing those emotions to the Lord.

Our wounds stay clean when we make Jesus our source and focus through the healing process. He has to be everything to us—the beginning, the end, and all that is in between. If this is not His place, then He takes no place at all.

Pain will fight to be the center of our attention, but pain itself provides no healing, no comfort, no sustaining power. Putting Jesus at the center of our healing means all other things fall into the periphery.

He comforts and exposes any infection that has developed through the web of lies we may be believing about our loss. He will treat it with the antiseptic of truth if we will be open to receive it, and then He binds up the wound to protect it as it heals. This takes time. For some it's shorter; for others it's longer. Either way, God is thorough and doesn't get in a rush. The silver lining is that we're moving forward while we're being healed.

A WORK OF ART

With intentionality, our pain can have purpose. We're the only ones with the right to decide if our suffering was for naught. But we can also choose to let our pain defeat the enemy by maturing us, bringing us closer to God, setting us free from hindrances, and by bringing God glory. And while that happens, something even more exciting will be going on. While we grow and heal, the Master will be remaking us. We won't be pieced together with hot glue and tape. We won't be hanging on by a thread. We'll become new works of art, finely crafted by His master skill.

There is a Japanese method called *kintsugi* that is used to repair damaged pottery. Rather than camouflaging the broken pieces with adhesive, kintsugi uses gold-dusted lacquer to fill the cracks. This method honors and values the brokenness and imperfection instead of concealing it. And with the added gold veins, the repaired piece is not only usable but more beautiful, unique, and valuable than it was before.

I suspect that God loves it when we admire the kintsugi work He's done in one of His children. His glory is displayed in the mended vessel, which boasts traces of shimmering gold along the cracks and fissures once caused by heartache. We are God's very own handiwork, His one-of-a-kind kintsugi design. He has repaired our pain with gold-dusted purpose. This is Christ's glory, Christ revealed through His children.

The fact that you're reading this book to learn how to move forward through your pain is God's glory alive in you. It's His power, love, strength, and grace revealed in your humanity—and mine.

These are the signs and wonders the world seeks. People are crumbling and desperate to know the God who is holding us together so beautifully. It's our mission to show them, and staying on this mission is how we turn our pain into purpose.

HERE ON PURPOSE

Corporately, as the body of Christ, our mission is to make disciples of Jesus in this world. But each one of us has a personal mission that is fleshed out uniquely in our own sphere of influence.

God handpicked you out of eternity and destined this time and space for you to be born. You are here on purpose. Look around and observe who is next to you. They are here on purpose too. Then consider: Where is your influence? What doors are already opened for you? Your starting place for your mission is wherever you currently stand and whomever you currently stand next to, whether it's bringing Christ's hope into a classroom, a church, a corporate office, or Starbucks while having coffee with a neighbor. That's something we all can do.

YOUR STARTING PLACE FOR YOUR MISSION IS WHEREVER YOU CURRENTLY STAND AND WHOMEVER YOU CURRENTLY STAND NEXT TO.

As we share our experiences, failures, and successes and give God praise for the way He's sustained us through them, others will be encouraged.

We can watch from up close or afar, take notes, and try to live out what we learn. This is how the body of Christ works. We live out loud, live authentically, live courageously, and then do it all over again. In vulnerability, observation, and participation, the body is strengthened.

Staying on mission keeps us from stalling in dysfunction and dying at the dead end of disappointment. It gives us direction instead of allowing us to wander in circles. It places a bull's-eye within our sight and gives our arrows a target. Without something to aim for, why try? Why not just toss down the arrow and drown our sorrows in a cup of something strong?

Don't let doubt and disappointment steal your mission. Make a practice of going to Jesus, emptying out your soul's pain, listening to His truth, and taking what you've learned to a world that is literally dying in hopelessness. If properly cultivated, our seeds of purpose that were planted in pain can grow into a harvest for the world to glean.

It is our choice what we will do with the miracle God is doing in us. I want to purposefully use mine every day to make His name great.

ELEVEN

ETERNAL PERSPECTIVE

The church auditorium was packed, and the energy in the room was palpable. It was obvious the women had shown up to She, Keypoint Church's annual women's conference, with an expectancy to encounter Jesus. The conference theme was Love on Fire, and our scripture had been carefully chosen to highlight our focus on the unrestrained love of God, which life's floods cannot drown out:

> Place me like a seal over your heart,
>   like a seal on your arm;
> for love is as strong as death,
>   its jealousy unyielding as the grave.
> It burns like blazing fire,
>   like a mighty flame.
> Many waters cannot quench love;
>   rivers cannot sweep it away.

(Song 8:6–7)

Unintentionally, this year's conference had been scheduled on the twentieth anniversary of Haven's eternal trade.

During the opening worship, as we sang about seeing victory in our lives, I felt the Holy Spirit say to me, *Use your story to tell them they will see a victory.* To be honest, I didn't want to do it. It was an emotional day for me, and I didn't want to break down, to make the conference or even that moment about me. So reluctantly I stayed in my place on the front row and continued to worship.

But God is relentless, isn't He? *Give them hope by giving Me glory.* He wouldn't let up, and my heart beat faster and harder until I finally obeyed and picked up the microphone, walked onto the stage, and spoke to the crowd. "I want you to know that no matter what you're facing, you will see a victory. I am a living, breathing testimony that the Lord takes what the enemy means for evil and turns it for good."

I paused for a moment and felt the Lord lead me to get vulnerable. "Twenty years ago today, Casey and I lost our firstborn daughter. For so many years I anticipated the anniversary of her death with dread— until the Lord showed me how to turn it around by asking Him to show me His goodness."

At that point the tears that I desperately didn't want to shed poured like torrents of rain. "Today as I drove here, there was a huge rainbow over my neighborhood. It reminded me of the faithfulness of God. You may see only part of the rainbow right now, but if you press on you will see it in full. There is a fulfillment to His promise. He is faithful.

"I would have never guessed as we battled for our daughter's life that I'd have the honor of standing here today giving God praise for what He's done. Can I tell you something? God makes good on His promises.

"You may be facing something that you think is going to kill you, but it will not. You have a Redeemer who is holding you together and an inner substance that is stronger than any trial Satan throws against you. Yes, the weapons will be wielded and the battle waged, but they will not conquer us. Instead, they will work for your good. And because of that, you will give God glory."

The atmosphere in the room shifted. Women wept, rejoiced, prayed for one another, and worshiped harder than I've seen anyone worship. And the undeniable presence of the Holy Spirit took over that room. He moved through the aisles, planting faith and renewing strength in open hearts. No one wanted to leave the room. That time was defining, not only for the conference, but for the women of Keypoint Church as well.

When I walked away from Haven's grave site twenty years ago, I could never have imagined the way God would use her death to give others hope: The teary-eyed wife I prayed for just last month whose husband was unfaithful. Or the brokenhearted mom I hugged who had lost her toddler in a swimming pool. Or the discouraged pastor's wife, who I looked in the eyes and told, "You can get through this."

Recently, a family friend who walked with us through that rough year with Haven told me something that brought me to tears. He said that in the last twenty years of practicing medicine, at least once a month he's told a patient about our story. It brings them hope, he said.

There's no way I could have fully seen the scope of lives that God would touch. There's no way any of us can imagine what God will do through our life's challenges. But during it all, "God use this!" was my cry. It was as if in that desire, my heart got a glimpse of what He could do, and that's what propelled me forward.

A LENS OF ETERNITY

If I had to pick one thing that has helped me come this far, I would say it is asking God to give me an eternal perspective, which biblical counselor Andrea Lee defines as "a way of seeing the pain, pleasure, and purpose of our lives as part of the redemptive story God is orchestrating. It is seeing *through* the daily grind, the tumultuous highs, and the frequent lows to the destination of eternity."[1]

PAIN IS NOT OUR END.
DOUBT IS NOT OUR END.
DISAPPOINTMENT
IS NOT OUR END.

Looking at life on earth as a pilgrimage to our forever home enables us to look through suffering to an unseen redemption that is sure to come. Pain is not our end. Doubt is not our end. Disappointment is not our end. It's so important that we remember this when we face trials. Through the lens of eternity, we have the divine ability to see higher. To "set [our] sights on the realities of heaven, where Christ sits in the place of honor at God's right hand" (Col. 3:1 NLT).

Why is life with an eternal perspective better than one without? Andrea Lee suggests:

> Without an eternal perspective, we misinterpret the details of our lives. Here's how that happens: we see anything that hinders our comfort and convenience in the present as a nuisance, or even an enemy. We despair over lost opportunities and frantically clamor for relational and physical fulfillment. We seek satisfaction for the infinite longings of our hearts by forcing, demanding, and manipulating our way through life. We misinterpret and reject hardship of all kinds because we don't have an internal view of God's eternal picture.[2]

Living with an eternal perspective helps us avoid those pitfalls because it helps us to see beyond our pain. Naturally speaking, you see, pain is opaque. When I stub my pinky toe on the metal leg of my coffee table, my entire body seizes until the pain subsides. That toe is the smallest appendage on my body, but it has the power to control me. In that moment, I can't see anything in my mind's eye or feel anything but the pain in my toe.

OUR PAIN MUST BE MADE TRANSLUCENT, SOMETHING WE LOOK *THROUGH* RATHER THAN LOOK *TO*.

For our lives to function the way God intends, however, our pain must be made translucent, something we look *through* rather than look *to*. And that's what a perspective of eternity can do. When we put on the lens of eternity, we can see through our present pain to a redeemed future. No matter what happens to us here on earth, we can have hope because heaven is our future home.

If You Could See Me Now!

"I love it," Casey said as he brushed away the tears spilling out of his eyes. That was exactly the reaction I was hoping for when he opened the Christmas gift I had bought him.

We were only two months removed from Haven's death, and this would be our first Christmas without her. Grief was still heavy, and disappointment still weighed on our hearts, so I'd wanted to present him with a gift that reminded both of us that there was hope beyond that painful place in time.

After a lot of searching, I had decided to frame Casey's favorite picture of Haven. I'd picked out a small silver frame that could sit on his desk and had it engraved with *Daddy, if you could see me now*.

I chose those seven words because to me they invoked an image of Haven healed, whole, and having a blast in heaven. I pictured her with long, thick brown hair, running barefoot through a field of wildflowers in a white dress, saying, "Keep going. Heaven is worth it!" That mental picture has helped me so much in those times when my eternal perspective dims and heaven feels far away.

The moment Haven passed away, I felt the closest to heaven I have ever felt. In one second, one crossing over of worlds, part of me was deposited in heaven. The presence of God settled in my bedroom like a weighted blanket, easing my grief. The veil shadowing my eyes thinned, and the other side felt more real to me than ever before. My heart connected with the world to come and felt its hope.

That heightened awareness of heaven lasted for months. Then, like the glow on Moses' face after spending time in God's presence (Ex. 34:29–35), it faded, and the veil thickened. But the seed of eternity in my heart is still growing free, wildly wrapping itself in every part of my soul. More than ever, my heart yearns for its glorious home.

> **IT IS CHRIST IN ME WHO SUPPLIES MY NEXT BREATH. AND IT IS CHRIST IN YOU WHO SUPPLIES YOURS.**

Life without Haven still occasionally snatches my breath away. Losing a child is rightfully excruciating, something that in many ways you never completely get over. Maybe you understand it all too well, but when I elevate my vision, as I'm compelled to do even today, and look through my pain to eternity, I realize that Haven was never the one who filled my lungs. It is Christ in me who supplies my next breath. And it is Christ in you who supplies yours.

Haven was a gift for me to steward, but she ultimately belongs to the Lord. My time on this earth with her was limited, but my time with her in heaven will be eternal. The joy that temporal things provide will come to an end. They momentarily satisfy but leave the soul empty. Setting our hearts on this present life is, to use Jesus' words, putting our treasure where thieves steal and moths and rust destroy (Matt. 6:19). Which is why we must strain to see eternity, that which lasts forever, and put our focus there.

WHAT'S ENOUGH

What is it that tempts you to believe that Christ isn't enough for you? If your husband doesn't stay, will you lose purpose? If your son makes one more mistake, are you afraid you're going to lose your mind? If your daughter gets pregnant in high school, will it shatter your dreams? If you lose your job, is everything going to crash down around you?

While a good marriage, wise children, and a stable job can help maintain life's peace, they are only a temporal source. We need something more stable, and we find it in Christ, in whom "we live and move and have our being" (Acts 17:28).

I want us to remind ourselves of this whenever we feel hopeless. We have to ask ourselves, *When did I start seeing Christ as less than I need? And what am I fixing my gaze upon that makes Him appear to me as less than enough?*

Whatever that focus is, it must be altered. Let us lift our eyes off the things of this world and look up to heaven. Let us remember that we are not servants, but sons and daughters of God, with direct access to the Most High, who embodies the answer to our every need and desire and longing.

GENERATIONAL PROMISES

God's promises may sometimes be the lighthouse seen shining at a distance, guiding us home through darkness and storms. Like Abraham, we may have some promises from God that we only see fulfilled at a distance with our spiritual eyes, for not everything is meant to be realized in our lifetime. God promised to make Abraham the father of nations, but it would take centuries for the "nations" to be birthed. Abraham was long gone by then, but the promise was fulfilled, and we are a fruit of the seed God planted in his soul.

God called Abraham out of Harran and gave him a vision of what was to come: a life in Canaan, God's promised land to him and his descendants. Then Abraham stood at a crossroads of decision. Would he move forward to an unknown place or stay where he was comfortably uncomfortable? Was Harran just as good as any place to live, or could he trust that what God had prepared was better than anything he knew?

When he picked up his family and belongings and moved onward, he got on with his purpose. No more waiting and hoping and wishing and wanting. It was time to go, and he heeded the call. Abraham wasn't born for Harran. He was born for the promised land. His choice affected so many more than just his immediate family. We are all reaping the benefit of his decision.

GOD IS GENERATIONAL, AND HIS PERSPECTIVE IS ETERNAL.

God is generational, and His perspective is eternal. He has the thirty-thousand-foot overview; naturally we see only what's in front of us. This is why we cannot expect to fully understand His ways in our lives. His ways are always higher than ours, and His plans are always better.

What if some of His promises to us now are seeds planted for future generations to reap?

What if what we think is a period is actually a comma in a sentence destined to continue on after we're gone?

Isn't that very thought enough to keep you moving forward into God's future?

Why It Is Well

You may be familiar with the old hymn "It Is Well with My Soul." The song was birthed from immense pain the writer, Horatio Spafford, endured in the late 1800s. Horatio lost his fortune in the Great Chicago Fire of 1871, shortly after losing his young son to illness. Then, in 1873, he sent his wife and four daughters ahead of him to Europe on the SS *Ville du Havre* with the promise to join them soon. But the ship sank while crossing the Atlantic, taking Horatio's four daughters down with it. His wife sent him a telegram with the words "Saved alone." Horatio boarded another ship to go to his wife, and it is said that when he passed the location where his family's ship had sunk, he penned the words of the hymn.[3]

"It Is Well with My Soul" has been loved by generations. In recent years I've seen "It Is Well" printed on everything from coffee mugs to T-shirts to human skin in the form of tattoos. But I'm going to be honest with you. When I hear that song, I don't always get a warm, fuzzy feeling. I certainly don't feel "it is well" about the loss of my child, and I'm not sure I ever will. Most of the time, in fact, "It ain't well" or "This sucks" more accurately describes my feelings. (I know I have just made the English teachers shudder, but sometimes proper words don't hold enough emotion to describe how you feel.)

It's okay that I will never be getting the T-shirt, because pain was never meant to signal "it is well" with us. But there is a bigger picture, which Horatio Spafford caught a glimpse of and which I am learning to see as well.

What makes all well with my soul is knowing *everything will be redeemed in the end.*

The apostle Paul eloquently opened up that bigger picture for us when he wrote:

> We do not lose heart. Though outwardly we are wasting away, yet inwardly we are being renewed day by day. For our light and momentary troubles are achieving for us an eternal glory that far outweighs them all. So we fix our eyes not on what is seen, but on what is unseen, since what is seen is temporary, but what is unseen is eternal.
>
> **(2 Cor. 4:16–18)**

That eternal perspective also grants me the ability to appreciate what my struggles have given me even here on earth. The maturing God has done in me through the pain, the voice of experience He's given me to encourage others, the deeper knowledge of who He is, the desperation that compels me to seek His face, not just His hand—*this, too,* is what is well with me. If I can trust Christ's wisdom in allowing the death of a child to be my experience, it is well with me.

And this is the same thing that can be well with you. Together we can join with our great cloud of witnesses and tell others how to overcome heartache and disappointment. We can show them our bruises and scars and tell them of our losses and heartache. We can speak of the times we made wrong choices and felt defeated and didn't know where to turn.

But we won't stop there. We'll also tell of the joy that we learned exists—joy that is greater than temporal happiness. We'll tell of what is waiting for us all on the other side of eternity. We'll tell of moments when God's grace met us at our lowest and put us back together with golden mortar.

We are better for what we've been through. We are on the winning side, and people need to know this hope.

I never imagined my heart would mend after losing a child. The gaping wound Haven's death left in me was filled with nothing less than Jesus. He helped me breathe again. He also gave me three more gorgeous children: Holland, Hayes, and Hudson. Though life isn't perfect, it is beautiful. Supernatural joy that I can't explain sustains me. It's not a temporary happiness but an internal strength that accompanies me through every hardship. My relationship with Jesus is still everything to me. He's my center. And I have had the privilege of speaking to anyone who would listen about the goodness and mercy of God.

THE GAPING WOUND HAVEN'S DEATH LEFT IN ME WAS FILLED WITH NOTHING LESS THAN JESUS. HE HELPED ME BREATHE AGAIN.

May it be our mission to create purpose from our pain. We must simply be determined not to let Satan win. If we keep following Jesus, we are on the winning side.

I've learned now, years removed from Haven's death, that it's worth every single hard-earned step that it takes to get here. So, today with God's grace, I choose again to commit the rest of my time on earth to overcoming everyday struggles, to nurturing the seed of eternity, stoking the fire of hope, pressing forward to obtain the crown and to receive the prize of heaven, our inheritance, that Jesus already won.

You are called to press forward too. When you gave your heart to Christ, you put your hands on a spiritual plow. Together with God and the body of Christ, you are called to plant seeds of righteousness throughout the earth. Let nothing distract you or hold you back so that you let go and walk away. Keep plowing, trusting, believing, and following Jesus. As God's sons and daughters in the body of Christ, we are cheering you on. We champion one another.

No matter what has happened to you in this life, if you are still breathing, you still have purpose. Your destiny didn't die with your dream. God never changed it. Don't quit on His promises or forfeit your inheritance, your life of victory, because you can't see your way out of disappointment. If you call out to Jesus, He will make a way for you.

The Christian life is a paradox, isn't it? A binary existence. Grief from one's pain and joy from Christ's redemption. The natural and supernatural. Mortal and immortal. Dance partners until the day we enter heaven. This is the goodness of God. We are promised that the negative side of life will be met with His presence. His joy colliding with weeping. The morning colliding with night. His company colliding with loneliness. Abundance colliding with lack. Grace colliding with ache.

In this paradoxical existence, instead of burying your hope, bury hopelessness. Instead of burying your devotion, bury your doubt and disappointment. Shovel the dirt on top of that grave, dust off your hands, and walk away. It's worth it.

If there is one thing I would like the opportunity to tell God's daughters—and you—it would be this: Don't give up. The battle is fixed. You've already won.

ACKNOWLEDGMENTS

To Andy Butcher for starting me on this journey.

To Janene MacIvor, Lauren Langston Stewart, Kristen Golden, and the rest of the team at Thomas Nelson. I cannot thank you enough for being so easy, patient, and enjoyable to work with. There's no doubt, you have to be the best in the business.

To Tiffany Martin for helping me organize the discussion guide. You helped keep me sane.

To my pastors, Larry and Melanie Stockstill. You built the house that built me.

To my parents. Thank you for loving me.

To Holland, Hayes, and Hud dawg. You are the greatest kids on the planet. The runners-up aren't even close.

To my friends that keep me laughing: Sandy Moreno, Kelly Niemeier, and Stacy Frye to name a few.

To my sisters-in-love: Stacey Hornsby and Samantha Morris. Family for life.

To my Keypoint Church staff. Wow. What a team. Specifically, Kelly Toney and Meagan Gay who assist me with life.

To Keypoint Church. Thank you for your love and faithfulness. To God be the glory!

NOTES

Introduction: Are We Stopping Too Short?

1. Note that different translations of the Old Testament spell the name of this city differently—some use "Harran," while others spell it "Haran." I have chosen to use "Harran" for several reasons: (1) It is the spelling used in the NIV, which is one of the primary versions I am using in this book. (2) It is the spelling used for the current-day city in Turkey. (3) It avoids confusion with the name of Terah's youngest son (also mentioned in this chapter), which is slightly different in Hebrew but often used interchangeably.

2. James Strong, *Strong's Exhaustive Concordance*, Bible Hub (website), s.v. "3427. Yashab" (Strong's H3427), accessed March 3, 2020, https://biblehub.com/hebrew/3427.htm.

3. *Strong's Concordance* H2771.

Chapter 2: Trusting Forward

1. Randy Alcorn, *Heaven* (Wheaton, IL: Tyndale House, 2004), 111.

2. C. S. Lewis, *The Lion, the Witch and the Wardrobe*, in *The Chronicles of Narnia*, combined ed. (New York: HarperCollins, 2004), 185.

3. Brené Brown, quoted in Dan Schawbel, "Brene Brown: How Vulnerability Can Make Our Lives Better," *Forbes*, April 21, 2013, https://www.forbes.com/sites/danschawbel/2013/04/21/brene-brown-how-vulnerability-can-make-our-lives-better/#7fe0dd8036c7.

4. *Strong's Concordance* H982.

5. Dictionary.com, s.v. "trust," accessed March 5, 2020, https://www
.dictionary.com/browse/trust?s=t.

6. J. A. Simpson and W. Fitch, "Locomotion," from *Applied
Neurophysiology* (1988), Science Direct (website), accessed March 6,
2020, https://www.sciencedirect.com/topics/neuroscience/locomotion.

Chapter 4: The Outline of His Presence

1. The internet term for "fear of missing out."

2. Charles H. Spurgeon, "No. 3150: Never, No Never, No Never,"
sermon delivered June 24, 1909, at the Metropolitan Tabernacle,
Newington, UK, in *The Complete Works of C. H. Spurgeon*, vol. 55:
Sermons 3125–3177 (Harrington, DE: Delmarva Publications, 2013).

Chapter 5: Joy That Heals

1. Tasha Eurich, "Laughter: The Surprising Secret to Surviving Tough
Times," *Huffington Post*, updated Dec. 6, 2017, https://www.huffpost
.com/entry/laughter-the-surprising-s_b_5651354.

2. Eurich, "Laughter."

3. Courtney E. Ackerman, "Positive Emotions: A List of 26 Examples
and Definition in Psychology," PositivePsychology.com, Oct. 25, 2019,
https://positivepsychology.com/positive-emotions-list-examples
-definition-psychology/.

4. Eurich, "Laughter."

Chapter 6: An Unlikely Weapon

1. *Strong's Concordance* G4352.

2. *Strong's Concordance* H7812.

3. *Strong's Concordance* H1984, H2167, H3034.

4. A. W. Tozer, *This World: Playground or Battleground: A Call to the Real
World of the Spiritual* (Wheaton, IL: Moody, 2017, orig. pub. 1989), 5–6.

Chapter 7: Theology Lessons

1. Wikipedia.com, s.v. "rat race," last modified Feb. 5, 2020, http://en
.wikipedia.org/wiki/Rat_race.

Chapter 8: Dealing with Disappointment

1. Dictionary.com, s.v. "distrust," accessed March 10, 2020, https://www
   .dictionary.com/browse/distrust?s=t.

Chapter 9: Even When He Doesn't Feel Good

1. Quick Reference Bible Dictionary, s.v. "good," Bible Study Tools,
   accessed March 12, 2020, https://www.biblestudytools.com/dictionary
   /good/.
2. Lewis, *The Lion, the Witch and the Wardrobe*, 146.
3. Carolyn Custis James, *When Life and Beliefs Collide: How Knowing
   God Makes a Difference* (Grand Rapids: Zondervan, 2001), 36.
4. Robert Madu, "Get Over It," sermon delivered at Elevation Church,
   Charlotte, North Carolina, 13:05, YouTube, posted June 24, 2019,
   accessed March 12, 2020, https://www.youtube.com/watch?v
   =lRVOJAmLDO4.

Chapter 11: Eternal Perspective

1. Andrea Lee, "Developing an Eternal Perspective," Radical (website),
   Nov. 30, 2018, https://radical.net/developing-an-eternal-perspective/.
2. Lee, "Developing an Eternal Perspective."
3. C. Michael Hawn, "History of Hymns: 'It Is Well with My Soul,'"
   Discipleship Ministries (website), June 2013, https://www
   .umcdiscipleship.org/resources/history-of-hymns-it-is-well-with-my
   -soul.

ABOUT THE AUTHOR

Stacy Henagan is a passionate pastor, speaker, author, and annual women's conference host. With more than twenty-five years of people-building experience, Stacy's weekly teachings offer inspiring biblical truth and practical application.

Stacy and her husband, Casey, are the founders of Keypoint Church in northwest Arkansas. They have four children: Haven, who they anxiously await to see again in heaven, and Holland, Hayes, and Hudson.